BUSINESS-TO-BUSINESS MARKETING

A STEP-BY-STEP GUIDE

BUSINESS-TO-BUSINESS MARKETING

A STEP-BY-STEP GUIDE

How to create sales, protect margins and build market share

Mark Eardley
Charlie Stewart

PENGUIN BOOKS

Published by Penguin Books
an imprint of Penguin Random House South Africa (Pty) Ltd
Reg. No. 1953/000441/07
The Estuaries No. 4, Oxbow Crescent, Century Avenue, Century City, 7441
PO Box 1144, Cape Town, 8000, South Africa

www.penguinbooks.co.za

First published 2016

1 3 5 7 9 10 8 6 4 2

PUBLISHER: Marlene Fryer
MANAGING EDITOR: Janet Bartlet
EDITOR: Christa Büttner-Rohwer
PROOFREADER: Dane Wallace
COVER DESIGNER: Sean Robertson
TEXT DESIGNER: Ryan Africa
TYPESETTER: Monique van den Berg
ILLUSTRATIONS: Rochelle van Wyngaard and Bianca Wykerd

Set in 11.5 pt on 15 pt Adobe Garamond

Printed by *paarlmedia*, a division of Novus Holdings

This book is printed on FSC® certified and controlled sources. FSC (Forest Stewardship Council®) is an
independent, international, non-governmental organization. Its aim is to support environmentally
sustainable, socially and economically responsible global forest management.

ISBN 978 1 77609 012 9 (print)
ISBN 978 1 77609 013 6 (ePub)
ISBN 978 1 77609 014 3 (PDF)

Contents

Introduction

Are you convinced your marketing is working?
- Is it generating sales?
- Is it protecting your margins?
- Is it building your market share?

This practical guide will help you make your marketing make money. It is about how to put marketing principles into practice to get results – in your business. It will help you create sales, protect your margins and build your market share.

To help you make sure that you can make this happen, we've included simple, practical tasks to get you into the fast lane to success – and keep you in it. We call these tasks 'Directions to results'. You'll find them at the end of chapters. They are an accurate, up-to-date GPS for B2B marketing. Follow the directions and you will get results.

The great thing about them is that they link up to build your marketing into a real money-making machine. That's because they're a sequence of steps that lead directly to profitable sales.

Marketing in the B2B environment

UNDENIABLY A SPECIALIST FUNCTION

WHAT IS B2B MARKETING?

Business-to-business or B2B marketing is sometimes referred to as industrial or trade marketing, and it deals with products and services that are bought by enterprises rather than individual consumers. For example, not many of us will ever buy earthmoving equipment or a conveyor belt for personal use or as a birthday present. And yet such things certainly are bought – even though you may not find them for sale in the stores you go to on a regular basis.

As consumers, we buy finished products that are ready to use and have been through all the processes they need to go through before they are finally put on the shelves. Very few of us still make our own shoes or clothes, and none of us would even think of making our own tyres.

B2B companies very often provide one element of a finished item. Their products and services are bought by other companies who use them in their products and services. Think, for example, of a cellphone and all its different elements. From the printing on its surface through to the battery inside, it contains a large number of parts that had to be changed from basic raw materials, by being manufactured, assembled, packaged and distributed as a brand new phone that is ready to be sold to consumers. If you consider all the parts and processes that go into *everything* that gets bought – either by enterprises or by consumers –

you will realise that they all add up to an astonishing amount of money being spent in B2B markets. In fact, the total B2B market is way bigger than the consumer market.

And that's why B2B marketing is so important.

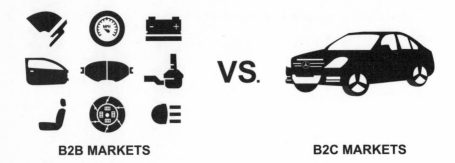

B2B MARKETS   **B2C MARKETS**

THE COMMERCIAL IMPORTANCE OF B2B MARKETING

Given that spending in B2B markets is far larger than *all* spending in consumer markets, it becomes clear that B2B marketing should be creating sales, protecting margins and building market share for your own company. It should be motivating your market to buy from *your* company and to keep on buying from *your* company. In other words: your B2B marketing should be a real money-making machine.

B2B MARKETING SHOULD MOTIVATE
YOUR MARKET TO BUY FROM *YOU*
AND TO KEEP ON DOING SO

We all recognise large consumer brands and understand that a great deal of money and effort goes into motivating us to buy them. These large brands certainly understand the power and importance of marketing. They put so much effort into their marketing that we see it and hear it all around us every day.

So why isn't the same kind of thing happening throughout B2B markets? Why is the power of marketing – and what it can achieve commercially – so badly neglected in the B2B environment?

Perhaps many B2B companies misunderstand the marketing function. Or perhaps its voice doesn't carry enough authority internally, and that's why not much happens on the marketing front. Maybe these companies don't see marketing as a profit-generating, business-sustaining function, and that's why they don't pay much attention to it.

Because there is certainly a common notion in many B2Bs: 'We don't do all that marketing stuff here.' There's also a view among many marketers that B2B is boring – that it's somehow more fun, more interesting and more challenging to be marketing fabric conditioner or financial services than earthmoving equipment or IT solutions.

Whatever the reasons, there's clearly a great deal to be gained from a change in attitude here. All B2B companies should be taking advantage of the potential to create sales, protect margins and build market share through a structured, disciplined approach to their marketing.

But before it can have a truly positive impact on your sales figures, market share and margins, you need to understand what B2B marketing is all about and how to make it work. The best place to start is by looking at the reasons why B2B is so different from business-to-consumer or B2C marketing.

B2B VS. B2C: THE MAJOR DIFFERENCES

B2B marketing is a very different animal from B2C marketing. However, B2B also has much in common with B2C. For starters, its overall goals are the same: to build sales volume, market share and margins. Moreover, many of its activities are very similar, advertising being an obvious example. So the misconception that there's not much difference between B2B and B2C is perhaps understandable. But consider the following: genetically, people are about 99.9 per cent the same. That's what makes us *what* we are: human beings, as opposed to other mammals such as whales or bears. It is that tiny 0.1 of a genetic percentage point that makes us *who* we are – it makes us individuals who differ widely from one another.

So although B2B and B2C marketing may appear very similar, they are completely different. But what are these differences?

ALTHOUGH B2B AND B2C MARKETING SEEM VERY SIMILAR, THEY ARE COMPLETELY DIFFERENT

Major vs. minor consequences

B2C typically deals with frequent low-price purchases, high volumes, simple products, short sales cycles, inflexible pricing and minor consequences.

There's not a lot at stake when we make most of our personal purchases, and we don't give them much thought. There is no structured consultation or fact finding, and there are no presentations, vendor assessments or long-term return-on-investment considerations when you buy a trolley load of groceries or cleaning products from your local supermarket. And if an item is out of stock, this is not usually a major problem. You can try another store or switch suppliers and brands really easily. And if you can't get it today, chances are you'll get it elsewhere tomorrow.

But in B2B, *everything* changes, because *B2B typically deals with infrequent high-price purchases, low volumes, complex products, long sales cycles, flexible pricing and major consequences.*

If your company wants to buy four earthmovers for really serious money, you will be going through a much more involved process than you would on your next visit to the supermarket. And there is a lot more at stake, because if you buy the wrong earthmovers, the consequences are rather more far-reaching than when you buy the wrong toothpaste. In addition, continuity of supply is much more important in a B2B transaction, as it will seldom be possible to switch suppliers at the drop of a hat.

B2B buying involves more people

Another major difference between B2B and B2C is that many more people will influence the buying decision. B2B customers – the enterprises that buy and use your products – are only one part of an *overall* market that may contain many different elements that influence buying decisions. The overall market might include distributors and wholesalers, turnkey solution providers, specialist consultancies or professions, support and service providers, analysts, commentators in the media, special-interest groups, standards boards and statutory regulators, trade associations and even the general public.

However, there are also people with different needs within your customers' organisations. And each of their specific needs must be fulfilled by your products, services and processes.

Here is a simple example of the different influencers within a customer. Let's say your company makes fabulously reliable earthmovers and that among your customers are companies that build roads. High levels of reliability that cut your earthmovers' downtime and so increase their productivity is a really attractive benefit for the sales director at a road-builder. Why? Because he can tell customers that higher productivity allows him to build roads faster and at a lower cost than his competitors. And because he can work faster, he has the opportunity to do more road-building deals. So he has the potential to make more sales and earn higher commissions. Reliability is also an attractive benefit for the road-builder's finance director. But for him, in addition to the attraction of increasing sales, reliability also translates into lower cost-of-ownership and a higher return on investment. This creates the potential to increase income, improve margins and raise profitability. So he can grow his performance bonuses.

B2C VS. B2B: WHAT YOU *WANT* VS. WHAT YOU NEED

Companies that make earthmovers advertise. Companies that make cars advertise. They advertise for the same reasons and are looking for the same commercial results. Their advertising may well be based on the same principle: grabbing your attention and boosting your interest in their product.

The advertisement for JCB shown here promotes the idea that hassle-free operation is one of the ways its big machines will help build the success of your business. Fair enough ...

By contrast, the B2C approach to advertising is often very different. In 2008, the BBDO advertising agency in Athens, Greece, produced a controversial print advert for previously owned cars from a well-known luxury brand. It featured a head-and-bare-shoulders image of a beautiful blonde woman, with the tag line, 'You know you're not the first.' The none-too-subtle message was that you don't need to feel second-rate because you are choosing second-hand (an internet search for the tag line will bring up the advert).

The fact that this used-car advert is so blatantly sexist highlights the point that much B2C promotion is poisonous and deceitful. One of the many problems this creates is that it affects our attitude to *all* forms of promotion and the extent to which we trust it – either as B2B buyers or B2C consumers. We'll get to grips with this particular issue in Chapter 9 (PR and B2B), when we look at the challenges of countering 'orchestrated lying'.

But for now, with an advert having attracted attention, what happens next?

Unlike the (exclusively male?) used-car buyer who may be looking for a symbol of status and personal prestige, people who purchase earth-moving equipment do so purely for business reasons, and not to improve their lifestyle or to reward and please themselves. So while B2C customers are mainly motivated by what they want as opposed to what they need, B2B customers *are not* motivated to buy solely for emotional or personal reasons.

In Chapter 3 (B2B's Big Five buying motivators), we'll look at the specific reasons that truly motivate B2B buying.

But first we need to look at how B2B markets work and how buying decisions are influenced and made. This is very important, as in B2B it is these decisions that generate your sales, your margins and your market share.

1

The big, big market

Coming up in this chapter:

- B2B markets are complex structures, so make them simpler
  - Who's who in your *overall* B2B market?
- The B2B sphere of influence: Who influences buying decisions?
  - Spot the targets in your sphere of influence
  - Populate your sphere of influence
- Targeting buying decision makers
  - B2B buying: it's strictly business – and it's really personal
  - Business buying decisions carry business consequences
  - Is fear the key? Or confidence?

B2B MARKETS ARE COMPLEX STRUCTURES, SO MAKE THEM SIMPLER

When an enterprise buys things such as heavy machinery or a mega data server, as opposed to stationery and toilet rolls, a host of people will typically be offering advice on making the right buying decision. Unlike B2C markets, B2B markets encompass many different elements that can influence customers' buying decisions.

Who's who in your *overall* B2B market?

Some of the elements that influence buying decisions in a B2B environment may not come from within the company at all. The influence may come from outsiders who are seen as reliable sources for gathering advice and information – perhaps from a user group or from articles in the specialist trade and business media. Or they might be people who have been hired by your customers as consultants to provide expert advice regarding the right buying decision.

There may also be elements within the *overall* market who have no direct, formal input into the decision-making process. They might not sit in your customers' meetings, but their opinions may have a great deal of clout. Labour unions or special-interest groups, such as environmentalists, are a case in point. So although all buying decisions are eventually taken internally within the customer organisation, you need to know the answer to at least two questions:

- What or who are the elements within your overall market?
- How do they influence buying decisions?

In order to understand how B2B decision making works, let me introduce you to what I like to call the 'B2B sphere of influence'.

THE B2B SPHERE OF INFLUENCE:
WHO INFLUENCES BUYING DECISIONS?

This diagram may help you visualise how B2B decision making works.

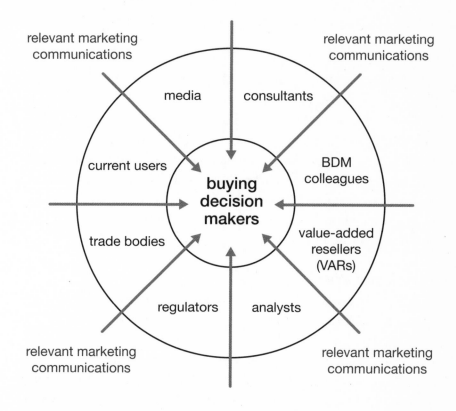

You will notice that the arrows in the diagram all point towards the centre: to the buying decision makers. So the combined weight of all the positive perceptions of everyone in the sphere needs to support a unanimous buying decision.

EVERYONE IN THE SPHERE MUST
SUPPORT THE DECISION TO BUY

In order to harness this support, it is essential that *all* influencers are exposed to relevant, credible information that addresses their specific concerns. Let's look at how you can use this diagram to define your influencers.

Spot the targets in your sphere of influence

The sphere-of-influence graphic shows clearly how buying decision makers within a customer organisation are typically surrounded by various influencers that make up the *overall* B2B market. There are two key points to bear in mind when you populate a sphere of influence:

- Each element of the overall market has an influence on your customers' buying decisions.
- Each element of the overall market is therefore an *audience* for your marketing messages.

Populate your sphere of influence

The first step towards building a marketing plan is to populate your sphere of influence.

While the sphere of influence can help you visualise who influences buying decisions, bear in mind that your particular market may include completely different audiences, and there may be more or fewer of them. Spheres of influence do differ: the sphere for a company that makes earthmovers will be different from that of an aircraft manufacturer. This means that you need to create your own sphere that shows *your* audiences, how they influence one another and the significance of their influence on your customers' buying decisions.

You may, in fact, find that individual customers need their own sphere that shows in detail how buying decisions are influenced and made within that particular organisation.

THE FIRST STEP TO BUILDING A MARKETING PLAN IS TO POPULATE YOUR SPHERE OF INFLUENCE

But let's not put the cart before the horse: you can only begin the process of creating messages that are *relevant* for each audience once you have an understanding of *who* these audiences really are.

The word 'relevant' is critically important here. For example, because there are multiple audiences within overall B2B markets, you cannot have catchy, one-size-fits-all brand messages.

Just as populating your sphere is a *structured* process, so is the business of creating relevant messages for *each* audience. We'll be covering this process in Chapter 5 (Content is king!). So while 'brighter than bright' may work for BriteRite washing powder, 'Just dig it' won't help you sell earthmovers to road-builders.

Focus on more than your customers

One thing that a sphere-of-influence diagram will show clearly is that buying decision makers do not operate in isolation.

An obvious example is the influence of the media. Most industry sectors have their own specialist publications – in print format, or digital, or both – that influence buying decisions. And many industries receive coverage in the business and general media, which can also influence decision makers. But unless you're selling some media-related product or service, media organisations are not your customers. They won't be buying your earthmovers. They can, however, certainly influence decision makers who do buy them, or might consider buying them. Consultants in the construction industry are also not going to be buying your earthmovers. But again, their influence may well carry more weight than what the media says about you.

Some of your audiences will have more influence than others. The significance of their influence can be plotted on your sphere to *guide* you when it comes to creating your marketing messages.

Once you have categorised *who* is in your overall market, you can decide on the targets for your marketing and ensure that all-important focus on buying decision makers.

TARGETING BUYING DECISION MAKERS

A good deal of your focus *will* be on customers and the decision makers within them. When you look at your sphere, it should make sense that whatever you're saying to customers needs to be the same as what the overall market is saying about you.

If each of the audiences in your sphere is saying that your earth-movers are absolutely fabulous, then your customers are likely to believe you when you tell them the same. It's music to a buying decision maker's ears if you *and* other audiences in the sphere are singing the same happy song in perfect harmony. It gives them a nice warm feeling, on a quite personal level.

WHAT YOU SAY TO YOUR CUSTOMERS NEEDS TO MATCH WHAT THE OVERALL MARKET SAYS ABOUT YOU

B2B buying: it's strictly business – and it's really personal

When we buy things as consumers, we might be motivated by some advertising and special offers or perhaps by rave recommendations from our mates. As consumers, we generally make our own decisions and stick to what we know and like. We buy what we want – not necessarily what we need.

However, in B2B, buyers need to be 100 per cent certain that their decision will be good for them. It is part of their job to make decisions that contribute positively to the success of their enterprise. If you buy the wrong toothpaste, it doesn't really matter too much. 'Why on earth did you buy that?!' is not such a dreadful question to answer when you get back home from the shops. But if a company buys the wrong data server or the wrong earthmover, answering the same question, particularly if it's the CEO who's doing the asking, carries a bit more bite.

Business buying decisions carry business consequences

Big decisions mean big consequences. Sometimes these consequences will be positive, but sometimes they won't. Whatever the consequences, the fact that there *will* be consequences is very significant to B2B marketers in two ways. First, does the overall market know that buying from your company definitely has happy consequences only? Secondly, do your customers' decision makers know the sad personal consequences of *not* buying from you?

NOBODY WANTS TO RISK THEIR CAREER OR THREATEN THE SUCCESS OF THEIR ENTERPRISE BY BUYING THE WRONG PRODUCT OR SERVICE

Is fear the key? Or confidence?

It has been said so often that some B2B marketers actually believe it: fear motivates business buying decisions – fear of the consequences that will rain down on the heads of boo-boo buyers. This might have been true before we entered the age of the information superhighway. But buying decision makers can now find out an awful lot about your products and services from the web.

The information superhighway serves one vitally important purpose for your customers: it allows them to build their *confidence* in your company and your products and services right from the start of the B2B buying cycle. We'll look at how that cycle works in Chapter 2 (Things *are* what they used to be: B2B's basic rules).

Creating your own sphere is essential, because it gives you the opportunity to target the right audiences in your overall market with confidence-building messages. Your sphere gives you a solid foundation for creating a positive influence on its centre: the buying decision makers.

For now, that's enough on the dynamics of the big, big market. You now need to take a step back and look at the fundamental rules that should be providing the direction for your B2B marketing.

DIRECTIONS TO RESULTS

In these sections at the end of each chapter, you will get into the fast lane towards creating profitable sales by following some clear directions to results. Let's start putting into practice – in your business – the principles covered so far.

Directions to results for Chapter 1 will show you:
- *who influences buying decisions for your customers and prospects*
- *who you need to target with your marketing activities.*

Follow these steps to get into the fast lane:
- Choose a major customer and create a sphere of influence that includes the names, job functions, responsibilities and contact details of people who influence that customer's buying decisions. As a guide, you can use the example of a sphere of influence on page 13 in this chapter. Remember to populate it with your influencers.
- Repeat the exercise for each key customer.
- Now look for similarities in who influences buying decisions. Do the same type of influencers keep appearing in each of your spheres? For example: finance, IT, production, outside consultants or the media?
- The last thing to add to your sphere is information on who you think has the most influence on buying decisions and the reasons why they have it.

These are really simple tasks. And although they're easy to complete, the knowledge you gain about your overall market is going to be pure gold later on.

2

Things *are* what they used to be: B2B's basic rules

MARKETS CHANGE, TECHNOLOGIES CHANGE,
PEOPLE CHANGE – BASICS DON'T

Coming up in this chapter:
- The basic rules of B2B marketing are still the same
  - 'The Man in the Chair'
  - B2B sales start way before the sales process begins
  - The B2B buying cycle and the impact of the information superhighway
  - Who's your competition?
  - Recession marketing? New-economy marketing?
  - Getting back to B2B basics
- B2B's three big, basic questions
  - Question 1: Who are you?
  - Question 2: What do you do?
  - Question 3: Why do you matter – to me, the customer?
  - The three Ps of B2B marketing: purpose, process, promise

THE BASIC RULES OF B2B MARKETING ARE STILL THE SAME

Markets change, technologies change, people change. Basics don't.

In 1958, American business magazines publisher McGraw-Hill ran a print advert, which has since become known as 'The Man in the Chair'.

'The Man in the Chair', McGraw-Hill magazines, 1958 (reproduced by permission of the McGraw-Hill Companies, © The McGraw-Hill Companies, Inc. No redistribution or reproduction without the permission of the McGraw-Hill Companies, Inc.)

'The Man in the Chair'

'The Man in the Chair' advert, created by advertising agency Fuller & Smith & Ross, is clear in its *purpose*: to promote B2B advertising in McGraw-Hill's business, professional and technical magazines. The questions it poses are as relevant today as they were almost sixty years ago: *Who are you? What do you do? Why do you matter?*

The message from the advert is also clear: you are what the market thinks you are. In other words, you get nowhere if the market doesn't know who you are, what you do and why you should matter to customers.

YOU'LL GET NOWHERE IF THE MARKET DOESN'T KNOW WHO YOU ARE, WHAT YOU DO AND WHY YOU MATTER TO CUSTOMERS

B2B sales start way before the sales process begins

The message from the Man in the Chair is actually even more important today than it was back in 1958. That's because information about B2B companies, their products and their services is now widely accessible from the information superhighway known as the internet.

The information on the internet is freely available without anyone having to make any direct contact with anyone from your company. You probably don't even know that this is happening. Without any input from you, the opportunities for customers to start the buying process are enormous compared to 1958. Customers are doing so online. And they are definitely doing it on their own.

From simple Google searches through to open-forum message boards, customers are building their first impressions and drawing conclusions about your company long before they even consider making personal contact with your sales team.

The result? Customers are selling to themselves. More and more, they are reducing the long-established influence of B2B sales teams. Information-enabled customers are self-educated, self-informed customers. And they are cutting your opportunities to sell to them.

The B2B buying cycle and the impact of the information superhighway

B2B buyers obviously need *confidence* in the decisions they are making. They want to avoid risk to themselves and to their organisation. The internet has enabled them to develop levels of confidence in a way that seems impartial and factual to them. It is enabling buying decision makers to form their own opinions and begin making choices *independently* of your sales team.

The B2B buying cycle graphic depicts the six phases of the buying process. It shows how the information that buyers need changes as they move from identifying needs through to buying whatever addresses those needs. Customers today can find out much about your business for themselves – particularly in the cycle's first three phases: identifying needs (phase 1), setting criteria (phase 2) and specific research (phase 3). They no longer need or want someone – possibly a complete stranger – to attempt to build their confidence in a face-to-face sales meeting.

The B2B buying cycle

Digitally savvy customers prefer selling to themselves because they don't want anyone else trying to sell them something. They'd much prefer to make up their own minds about what they need and where to buy it. Businesses have become increasingly comfortable with finding out what they need on their own. They're happy to fly solo through the cycle's first three phases, and it's increasingly likely that customers and prospects see no reason to contact you directly. They're much happier selling to themselves, online and on their own.

CUSTOMERS ARE HAPPY TO SELL TO THEMSELVES, ONLINE AND ON THEIR OWN

This is why understanding what's happening in the B2B buying cycle is very important. In Chapter 5 (Content is king!), we'll look at the buying cycle in detail, and at the type of information you need to provide for each of its six phases. But for now, let's get back to the information super-highway and look at another impact that it's having on B2B marketing: dealing with your competitors.

Who's your competition?

You may think you know who your competition is. But there may be a lot more competition out there than you realise. The internet has dramatically raised *expectations* about the accessibility of information. Think about the way you use the internet and what you expect from it. Information that is relevant, clearly laid out and easily accessible is far more useful than, say, a website with limited or faulty functionality, no relevant information and an annoying form to complete before you can even request the information you need. When you can't find what you need, you'll look for it somewhere else.

This means that if buyers can't find what they need from your business online, they will look elsewhere. And that's where their money will go: elsewhere.

So if you want to stay ahead of the competition and want to stop potential buyers from taking their money elsewhere, it's now more important than ever to provide your market with information that is visible, credible and relevant. Why? There are two reasons: you need to be heard, and you need to beat the bad times.

IF BUYERS CAN'T FIND WHAT THEY NEED ONLINE, THEY'LL LOOK ELSEWHERE

Getting heard

First of all, there are so many marketing messages out there, delivered over so many different platforms, that you need to make sure that *yours* are the ones that get seen and heard and will motivate buyers to buy. The crux here is not that your messages need to be heard more clearly than those of your *direct* competitors: you need to be aware that many companies with completely different products and services are also trying to get their messages heard by your customers.

All those companies are after the *same* things as you: budget allocations and the purchase orders that go with them.

So you need to stand out from *all* the competition.

A company that produces earthmovers will be targeted by multiple suppliers of different products: engines, tyres, transmissions, hydraulic systems, brakes, windscreens, prefabricated steel, electronics, nuts and bolts, paints, lubricants, and machine and hand tools – as well as canteen and washroom facilities and IT solutions. Standing out from this crowd is a lot more complicated than standing out on a supermarket shelf!

B2B marketers are really competing for their audiences' time. You want a higher share of their attention than all the other companies that are targeting them.

Beating the hard times

The second reason why it's important to provide visible, credible and relevant information is that times are hard. We're in the midst of a global downturn. Money is tight and we are all competing for slices of a shrinking pie.

This situation, more than anything else, underlines the importance of sticking to B2B's basic rules.

Recession marketing? New-economy marketing?

Difficult times create difficult B2B marketing demands: Generate sales! Build market share! Protect margins! Cut marketing costs and increase return on investment (ROI)! Get closer to customers! Reinforce relationships! Innovate! Drive the brand! Boost visibility! Neutralise competitors! Refresh the message! Take cover!

With one obvious exception, doesn't this list include the things marketing should be doing *all* the time?

So why is there such a bright spotlight on them when times are hard?

If your products and services cut customers' operating costs, do they become more attractive in a recession? If so, were they somehow *less* attractive pre-recession?

Could it be that in good times customers don't think about reducing their operating costs in order to protect their margins or boost sales by offering more competitive pricing? Surely not?

Check the web and you'll find stacks of information on how marketing should respond to a recession. In early 2008, before the jaws of the global recession had really started to bite, a Google search on the exact phrase 'recession marketing' returned 59 600 results. By November 2009, the same search got over 13 million results. By late 2015 that figure had jumped to a staggering 41 million results.

IS CUTTING COSTS
ATTRACTIVE IN A RECESSION?
WAS IT LESS ATTRACTIVE
BEFORE THE RECESSION?

Recession marketing? New-economy marketing? There are no such things!

Getting back to B2B basics

In 2008, fifty years after 'The Man in the Chair' advert first appeared, the Business Marketing Association in the US staged an anniversary live version of the advert (more about this at the end of this chapter). It's absolutely essential viewing because it shows that the fundamental rules – the basics – of B2B marketing are the same now as they were back in 1958.

All the talk about 'recession marketing' and 'new-economy marketing' centres on getting back to basics. This is a signed confession that a lot of B2B marketing had lost its way and wasn't creating sales, protecting margins or building market share. Which is, of course, what it always should have been doing.

B2B equals 'back 2 basics' here: the back-to-basics rules should drive your B2B marketing when the good times roll *and* when they don't.

So how can you get back to basics?

B2B EQUALS 'BACK 2 BASICS'

B2B'S THREE BIG, BASIC QUESTIONS

Getting back to basics boils down to answering three big, basic questions the market still asks:

- Who are you?
- What do you do?
- Why do you matter – to me, the customer?

The Man in the Chair highlighted these three basic questions way back when. They still dominate B2B marketing. And they still need answering in a way that builds confidence in your company, your products, your services and your processes. Most importantly, the market needs to believe your answers. It needs to be confident that your answers are credible and that you can be trusted.

So, let's look at how you might want to formulate your answers and generate that sales-creating trust.

Question 1: Who are you?

Why do you need to answer this first question? Because, as the Man in the Chair says: *I don't know … your company or your reputation.*

He is saying: I don't know what makes you different from everyone else in the market. What is it about your company that *shows* how you are different from competitors?

The answer to this question is based on how your company operates, how it is experienced in the market, and gives the reasons why customers should buy from you – instead of the competition.

Defining this difference is often a particularly difficult challenge for B2B companies.

It helps to think about it like this: We are all different. Just as no two people are the same, no two companies are the same. As individuals, we often take most for granted what we're most capable of doing.

How many CVs are a true reflection of what a person can do *and* how they do it? Not many, I'd say. The same goes for companies. Take a look at all your sales and marketing material. Is it a true reflection of how your company builds the success of its customers? Does it generate the sales-creating trust that will motivate customers to buy from you? Or is it filled with a lot of brochure-speak, like 'outcomes-oriented technologies', 'acute customer focus', 'enhanced feature-to-benefit ratios' and 'superior service excellence'? Is it more about what your company *thinks* it should be instead of what it really is?

And here's the real nightmare question: *Is your logo the only thing that differentiates you from the competition?*

IS YOUR LOGO THE ONLY THING THAT DIFFERENTIATES YOU FROM THE COMPETITION?

Jack Trout, an internationally respected US marketing consultant, stresses the critical importance of being seen as different:

> *Differentiate or die. In our killer competitive economy, if you don't have a point of difference, you'd better have a very low price.*
> – Jack Trout

Question 2: What do you do?
Why does this second question need an answer? Because, as the Man in the Chair says: *I don't know ... your products and your services.*

He is saying: I don't know what your products and services can do for *me*.

Many B2B companies sell the same type of products or services, and all appear to be doing pretty much the same thing. Why should the market be motivated to buy what you're offering?

You need to know and show how your products and services make a positive contribution to the continuing success of your customers.

YOU NEED TO SHOW HOW YOUR PRODUCTS AND SERVICES CONTRIBUTE TO THE SUCCESS OF YOUR CUSTOMERS

You need to define clearly how all the features of your products and services translate into benefits that are relevant to your customers. You need to identify *all* the successes produced by these features.

This question is most certainly *not* about 'world-leading products' or 'customer-centricity', or any of the other meaningless blah-blah-blah that pads out much of the 'uniquely positioned' B2B marketing you might have seen.

So remember: Your products, your services, your processes – what will they do for ME?

Brochure-speak: thought-leading, fast-tracking rubbish-speak

Just for a laugh, here's an old classic on how easy it is to create brochure-speak. It's called the buzz-phrase generator and is generally accredited to the Canadian Department of Defence from around forty years ago. This version is taken from the book *The Complete Plain Words*, by Sir Ernest Gowers.

Here's how it works: you choose three numbers from 0 to 9 and build your own phrases that might sound fabulously significant but will actually mean zero to your customers.

For example: 745 gives you 'synchronised digital concept', and 561 produces 'responsive transitional flexibility'. Neat, isn't it?

My car number plate provides 'balanced digital capability', and my old street number throws up 'overall organisational flexibility' – which I consider particularly apt since I no longer live there.

And the 463 from my cellphone number is absolutely spot-on: 'functional transitional mobility'. Try it yourself!

0. integrated	0. management	0. options
1. overall	1. organisational	1. flexibility
2. systematised	2. monitored	2. capability
3. parallel	3. reciprocal	3. mobility
4. functional	4. digital	4. programming
5. responsive	5. logistical	5. concept
6. optimal	6. transitional	6. time-phase
7. synchronised	7. incremental	7. projection
8. compatible	8. third-generation	8. hardware
9. balanced	9. policy	9. contingency

Of course, no truly professional B2B marketer would ever dream of using such useless phrases. Or would they?

> *Jargon? It is not English, except in the sense that the words are English words.* — Sir Ernest Gowers

> *Our business is infested with idiots who try to impress by using pretentious jargon.* — David Ogilvy

These two statements might seem overly harsh, but if you think about them in terms of 'brochure-speak' there's more than a grain of truth in them!

Question 3: Why do you matter – to me, the customer?

Why does question 3 matter? Because, as the Man in the Chair says: *I don't know … your track record and what you achieve for your customers.*

The answer to this question demonstrates how you support your customers' success and retain their loyalty. It defines the reasons why existing customers choose to keep on buying from you.

What does your company achieve for its customers? How does it contribute to their continued success? Where is your proof that your company should matter to my company?

Simply listing your customers doesn't do the job here – no matter how big and impressive they may be. After all, would you automatically buy something from another company *only* because they supply some well-known enterprises? It's much more important to explain *how you work with* customers, *how long* your company has dealt with them and *how you contribute* to their successes.

Case studies and testimonials are far more relevant than a list of big-name customers and big-money deals. Of course, your case studies and testimonials need to be relevant to the various audiences in your B2B market.

There's not much to be gained by telling a road-builder how fabulous you are at mining *unless* you can clearly show that your business processes – as well as your products and services – are commercially relevant to both industries.

Finally, are you here to stay? Financial stability and your plans for the future go a long way towards answering questions about your ability to provide long-term success for customers.

The three Ps of B2B marketing: purpose, process, promise

These three big, basic questions and how you answer them should always be at the forefront of your mind. An easy way to keep them there is to think of them as the three Ps of B2B:

- Purpose: This is the 'Who' – Who are you? Who is your company?
- Process: This is the 'What' – What do you do, and how are you able to do it?
- Promise: This is the 'Why' – Why do you matter to me, the customer? And why should I buy from you?

Keeping the three Ps – purpose, process and promise – topmost in your thinking is also important as we look at what *motivates* B2B buying. Which is precisely what's coming up in Chapter 3 – B2B's Big Five buying motivators.

MORE ABOUT 'THE MAN IN THE CHAIR' ADVERT

Here's some more information about 'The Man in the Chair' advert, and the agency that created it, Fuller & Smith & Ross (FSR):

- 'In 1958, FSR created one of the great classics of business-to-business advertising for McGraw-Hill Publishing Co. The print ad pictured an executive in a bow tie, hunched forward in a swivel chair, and scowling into the camera. It was an image that represented every salesman's worst nightmare when making a cold sales call. The ad was conceived by FSR account exec, Gilbert Morris, who initially posed for the picture to convey the kind of look he wanted in the final ad. His forbidding image fit so perfectly that he ended up using himself in his own ad' (extract from *Advertising Age* magazine, www.adage.com).

- In 1999, *Advertising Age's Business Marketing* named it the best business-to-business advert of the 20th century.

- The live, updated version of 'The Man in the Chair' advert, staged by the Business Marketing Association in 2008, can be viewed here: www.youtube.com/watch?v=nXG7zYWKHGU.

DIRECTIONS TO RESULTS

You can now start to apply B2B's basic rules in your business by addressing the critical questions that all customers and prospects want you to answer. You can then begin the process of generating sales-creating trust throughout your market. And that's really important.

Directions to results for Chapter 2 will show you:
- *how to answer the big, basic questions that all B2B customers and prospects ask*
- *how to begin the process of describing your business in ways that will be consistently relevant to your market – so that it will be motivated to buy from you.*

Follow these steps to get into the fast lane:
- Write a description of about fifty words for each of your three Ps (your purpose, your process and your promise). As you write them, bear in mind that your descriptions must answer the big, basic questions covered on page 29: *Who* are you? *What* do you do? *Why* do you matter to customers?
- Check with your colleagues in other departments (sales, finance, production) whether they agree with the descriptions you wrote. Can they add anything more that they believe is relevant to customers?
- Run a 'jargon check' on all your sales and marketing material. Then make a note of any meaningless stuff that sounds as if it was produced by a buzz-phrase generator. You're going to get rid of it smartly when we sort out your marketing content in Chapter 5.

3

B2B's Big Five
buying motivators

WHAT REALLY MAKES BUSINESS CUSTOMERS BUY

Coming up in this chapter:
- B2B's Big Five buying motivators: the five factors of value
  - What *is* value? It's what B2B customers buy
- Defining the Big Five
  - The five factors of value: response, service, time, quality, price
  - The obsession with price
- The Big Five in action
  - 'A horse! A horse! My kingdom for a horse!' – how value motivates buying decisions
  - Understanding the nuts and bolts of your customers' business
  - How do you contribute to your customers' success?
- Get out into the market and start talking to it
  - Be relevant, be credible
  - Be more direct – be much more direct

B2B'S BIG FIVE BUYING MOTIVATORS: THE FIVE FACTORS OF VALUE

Value is not a soft issue. It is tangible. It can be defined and it can be measured. There are five factors of value that motivate B2B buying: response, service, time, quality and price.

These five factors are the Big Five motivators of buying decisions

What *is* value? It's what B2B customers buy

If you want to *motivate* buying, then you need to demonstrate how your products and services deliver on the Big Five buying motivators: response, service, time, quality and price (an easy way to remember them is to think of them alphabetically, as PQRST). All B2B products, services and processes can be described in terms of these five factors.

ALL B2B PRODUCTS CAN BE DESCRIBED IN TERMS OF THE BIG FIVE

DEFINING THE BIG FIVE

It is important to keep the specific definitions of the five factors of value in mind as you begin the process of describing how you create value and motivate buying. It might help to think of these factors as *expectations* that your customers will have of your company.

The five factors of value: response, service, time, quality, price
Let's look at each of the Big Five in turn.

1. Response
- Continual dialogue with customers; listening systematically to how you can build their success
- Identifying and meeting your customers' changing needs
- Solving problems and delivering solutions speedily

2. Service
- Accessibility; an open and reassuring organisation
- Clear information on products, services, processes and project status
- Proactive and innovative service

3. Time
- Competitive lead times
- Dependable
- Consistent delivery format

4. Quality
- Consistent products, services and processes
- Meeting the brief or specifications reliably; providing fit-for-purpose products
- Achieving the customer's goals

5. Price
- Clear
- Competitive
- Structured
- Rational

While I said that an easy way to remember the five factors is alpha-betically, as PQRST, the Big Five have a specific order of importance. *Response* is always at the top of the list. And *price* is at the bottom. Which brings us to the obsession with price.

The obsession with price

Of the Big Five, price carries the simplest definition, is the easiest to understand and should be the easiest to communicate.

Price needs to be clear, competitive, structured and rational. That's all.

But since price is actually the least complex of the Big Five buying motivators, you need to think about this tricky question: Why all the fuss, all the time, about price?

'How much?' should be the simplest question to answer.

It might be forty bucks or it might be forty million. But that's what it is: a number!

As consumers, we usually don't even have to ask 'How much?' – the price is shown either on the price tag or it's displayed on the shelf. In fact, if the price is not clear, this annoys us. It might annoy us to the point where we *won't* buy the item.

But in B2B we tend to forget this. We make the simplest question the hardest to answer. Like this:

Question: How much?   Answer: Er, that depends ...
Question: On what?   Answer: Er, well, on lots of things.
Question: Such as?   Answer: Er, well, lots of things ...

Perhaps the reason for this is that in the world of B2B, products and services are more complex and consist of far more variables than in the B2C world.

For example, the unit price of a single item will probably be higher than the unit price for a hundred items; volume discounts are a common feature in B2B pricing.

Equally, there may be a number of service options that are allied to a product and affect its price, warranties being a fairly typical example.

Nevertheless, much like other consumers, B2B buyers expect clarity on price. And there is no reason at all why you can't provide a clear price. So the first thing about price is that it needs to be *clear*.

THE FIRST THING ABOUT PRICE
IS THAT IT NEEDS TO BE CLEAR

Secondly, the price needs to be *competitive*. It needs to be in line with what your competition is offering the market. This is an issue of *comparison*. So you need to ask yourself how everything about your products and services compares to your competitors.

That may sound straightforward. At first glance, it might appear that what you're providing the market is exactly the same as everyone else. But if you dig beneath the surface, you will definitely find differences.

In fact, you might find some *big* differences. You may find either that you are offering more for the same price or that you are offering less for the same price than your competition. The important thing is to understand what these differences are. I will help you build your understanding of this aspect later in this chapter through a story of a king and his horse.

The third component of price in B2B is that price must be *structured*. It must include features that cater for issues such as volume discounts, payment terms, service levels and allowances for special projects, testing or evaluations.

And finally, price must be *rational*. Buyers must see – and fully understand – the *reasons* why your price is what it is.

PRICE IS A MECHANISM OF EXCHANGE
FOR THE OTHER FOUR FACTORS OF VALUE

The obsession with price – 'It's too much!' – only comes into play when it's not clear *how* you are creating value in terms of the other factors of value – when your customers cannot see the price as rational.

Price is a needle on a gauge that measures how the other four value factors contribute to your customers' success.

Sadly, all too often, the market sees very little value beyond price and price alone. How the other four factors contribute to your customers' success is routinely ignored or taken for granted. This is when price becomes a blinding problem.

PRICE IS A NEEDLE ON A GAUGE THAT
MEASURES HOW MUCH YOU CONTRIBUTE
TO YOUR CUSTOMERS' SUCCESS

THE BIG FIVE IN ACTION

'A horse! A horse! My kingdom for a horse!' – how value motivates buying decisions

In the Shakespeare play *Richard III*, King Richard's horse is killed in battle and he is forced to continue fighting on foot. In desperation, he cries out:

'A horse! A horse! My kingdom for a horse!'

Let's consider what he is crying out for. For a moment, let's think of King Richard as a customer. At this very desperate moment, what is it that Richard needs – in terms of the Big Five buying motivators: response, service, time, quality and price?

Above all else he wants *response*. He needs to know that someone's listening and that they can solve his problem – that they can get him a horse.

As for *service*, does he need status reports telling him that the horse will definitely arrive before close of battle today? Probably not!

Time definitely matters to Richard. Although he doesn't say *when* he needs a horse, you know he wants it *right now*. Not later, but *now*, with an exclamation mark!

Is Richard really bothered about the *quality* of the horse he needs? Well, no and yes. He is not interested in all its features. He couldn't care whether it's a carthorse or a racehorse, armoured or saddled. Or whether it's a grey mare or a black stallion. In terms of *quality*, a living horse with a bit of go left in it will achieve Richard's goal. And that goal, right now, is to speed up the process of finding and ending the life of a bloke called Henry Tudor who thinks *he* should be king. But Richard definitely doesn't want a dead horse (he's already got one of those).

Finally, in terms of the Big Five, what does the desperate king say about *price*? It's as clear as daylight: Richard claims that he'll hand over his kingdom for a horse. Price is really not an issue for him at that particular instance. Of course, under normal circumstances, horses don't sell for the price of an entire kingdom. But if you're a king in danger of losing your crown for the lack of a horse, things change. So, you need to remember that what customers value changes according to circumstances.

WHAT CUSTOMERS VALUE CHANGES
ACCORDING TO CIRCUMSTANCES

This story of King Richard shows us the importance of:
- understanding your customer
- the context of the challenges they're facing, and
- how you can contribute to their success.

The last thing King Richard shows us is this: customers don't always spell out *exactly* what it is they need. So *you* need to find out what it is. You need to *understand* your customers and their particular challenges. Then you can tell them how you can *help* them.

Understanding the nuts and bolts of your customers' business

What do B2B customers need? They need success. This is indisputable. They need products and services that make positive contributions to the success of their organisation.

Let's consider a company called NuBoCo, which makes nuts and bolts, and one of its customers, AirCo, which builds aeroplanes. For NuBoCo to make a positive contribution to AirCo's success, they will also need to offer the following to AirCo:
- matched and packaged nuts and bolts
- adequate stockholding
- structured discounts
- nationwide or international delivery services
- approved dealer networks
- technical advice and training
- accounting services and credit facilities

- stock control and monitoring
- certifications and warranties
- product development and R&D.

CUSTOMERS WILL SELDOM SPELL OUT EXACTLY WHAT IT IS THAT THEY NEED. YOU NEED TO FIND OUT WHAT IT IS

Why does AirCo need all these things?

Here are some Big Five reasons *why* AirCo is buying from NuBoCo:

- If the bolts fail, the engines fall off. That would be disastrous! *Quality* is critical for us, because it ensures safety. That's why we buy NuBoCo's range of Aerospace Certified Equipment (ACE) products.
- Without these nuts and bolts, we can't put the wings on. And then we can't sell planes. That would also be the end of us! *Time* is critical for us because it creates continuity in our manufacturing and sales. That's why we signed a Minimum User-Supply Terms (MUST) contract with NuBoCo.
- Our customers around the world can't maintain their planes without these nuts and bolts. That hurts them *and* us. So, *service* is vital to us and to our customers. That's why we work with NuBoCo's channel of Accredited International Dealers (known as AID).
- Our next generation of planes will build our sales, strengthen our market share and protect our margins. But unless we get some new types of nuts and bolts, we can't make the planes and stay ahead of our competition. And that would be catastrophic. *Response* is critical and that's why we're signed-up with NuBoCo's Research and Modernisation Programme (RAMP).
- *Price* is obviously important to us. With NuBoCo, we know that every cent is wisely spent. We owe much of our success to the fact that they understand the nuts and bolts of our business as well as their own.

How do you contribute to your customers' success?

It's pretty clear that the supporting services offered by NuBoCo maximise their contribution to AirCo's success. NuBoCo is ticking all the right boxes in terms of the Big Five by providing different named and packaged services that motivate AirCo to buy their nuts and bolts.

In the same way as NuBoCo understands AirCo's needs, you need to understand how *every* aspect of your products, services and processes contributes to your customers' success. This means that you need to know how customers use your products, services and processes.

YOU NEED TO KNOW EXACTLY HOW CUSTOMERS USE YOUR PRODUCTS, SERVICES AND PROCESSES

Always keep in mind that the Big Five are what motivate customers to buy:

- response
- service
- time
- quality
- price.

So to get back to what you learnt from King Richard: Richard's need for a horse shows the importance of demonstrating the positive performance of your products and services in the *context* of current challenges. This is a continuous process that needs to be in tune with your B2B environment and how it's changing.

Sometimes the environment is relatively stable and the pace of change is moderate. This means your marketing messages can also remain stable.

But sometimes the pace and scale of change is far greater.

The current recession has certainly altered what customers value (and don't forget that this recession won't be the last). Any recession-battered enterprise will be particularly interested in how you can help them to:

- increase their efficiency
- cut costs
- protect their margins and market share.

Recession polarises market demands and B2B buyers all want the same thing. This means there is now greater uniformity in the challenges facing B2B marketers.

This translates to greater uniformity within marketing messages. Everyone is saying the same things. Or they certainly should be if they want to motivate buying in tough times. So your messages must be more visible, more credible and more relevant than ever before.

IN TOUGH TIMES, YOU NEED TO BE MORE VISIBLE, MORE CREDIBLE, MORE RELEVANT

GET OUT INTO THE MARKET AND START TALKING TO IT

In order to communicate messages that are relevant and credible in terms of the Big Five, you need to understand your customers' operations and their commercial environment.

Unless you are regularly interacting with people who influence and make buying decisions, you limit your ability to be seen as relevant and credible quite severely.

You can't interact with customers while sitting at your desk.

You need to meet customers and listen to how their business works.

Be relevant, be credible

Too many people who directly affect the customer experience often remain rooted in their offices, developing little understanding of what is happening within and around their customers and how buying decisions are being motivated.

Instead, they build their opinions on independent research and second-hand information filtered through to them from sales departments and customer-support teams.

This just ain't good enough.

Everyone who has an effect on the buying decisions that create your sales, protect your margins and build your market share has to get out and about, and circulate among *all* the audiences in their *overall* market and the sphere of influence that we looked at in Chapter 1 (The big, big market).

They *all* need to discover what the market is thinking, how it's responding to the challenges it faces and how your products and services are *relevant* to it. Because if you don't understand what's happening in the overall market and *why* you're relevant, how can you hope to convince anyone that what you are saying is *credible*?

So start accompanying salespeople when they visit customers, initiate activities that create opportunities for interactions with influencers, and build relationships with your industry's media and commentators.

But I can hear you thinking: Surely, that's what the sales team is supposed to do?

Yes. But you have to cooperate with your colleagues from other parts of your organisation. Do it together. As a team.

We'll be looking at this essential attitude of sales-creating cooperation – throughout your organisation – and how to motivate it, in Chapter 8 (Marketing united). For now, keep in mind that *anyone* who affects the customer experience needs to be meeting customers and finding out how to advance their success.

ALL WHO AFFECT THE CUSTOMER EXPERIENCE SHOULD MEET CUSTOMERS TO FIND OUT HOW TO ADVANCE THEIR SUCCESS

Be more direct – be much more direct

If you're marketing toothpaste, it's simply not practical to have direct contact with all your customers. But if you are producing the machinery that makes the toothpaste, your audiences are much smaller and far better defined.

While this is not the case in B2C, in B2B there are many opportunities to address buyers and influencers directly.

Direct interaction is therefore not only more practical in B2B – it is also one of the most effective tools in the sales and marketing toolbox.

As marketers are pressured to reduce spend, it's worth considering ways in which budgets can be used to create more direct contact with all the audiences that influence buying decisions.

It's a great opportunity to become more proactive. Which means that you can create your own contact points with your audiences as opposed to relying exclusively on established communication channels.

YOU NEED TO DRIVE COMMUNICATION CHANNELS INSTEAD OF BEING A PASSENGER

You need to be driving the communication channels instead of being a passenger.

- For example, you might organise events that focus on specific audiences as one way of taking greater control.
- If there's a need to reach finance directors, can you create a regular event that will motivate their attendance – perhaps a workshop on new legislation, market trends or forecasts?

- Instead of waiting for your sector's one big annual trade show, are there ways to organise something similar, but more specific and on a smaller scale?
- You could also find partners in media or industry associations to co-sponsor and promote such events.

We'll be looking at how to be more direct across a variety of communication channels in Chapter 7 (Extra special delivery).

But right now we need to get back to the Big Five buying motivators. We need to look at how to *apply* the principles of value in your marketing.

In the next chapter we're going to look at working with buying motivators.

BE MORE PROACTIVE: CREATE YOUR OWN OPPORTUNITIES

DIRECTIONS TO RESULTS

In this chapter you need to examine how you create value for customers. This may take a little time, but it will be time well spent – because you are now starting to deal with why customers should be motivated to buy from you.

Directions to results for Chapter 3 will show you:
- *the differences between what you're selling and what the competition is selling – and how your prices really compare on a like-for-like basis*
- *how to think about your products and services in terms of creating value for customers.*

Follow these steps to get into the fast lane:
- Make a list of the Big Five motivators and their definitions, and keep it somewhere visible, because you're going to use it regularly from now on.
- How competitive are your prices? How do they compare to your competition's prices? Most importantly, in terms of how they contribute to your customers' success, make a list of how your products and services *differ* from those offered by the competition.
- Choose one customer and list *all* the ways in which your products and services contribute to their success (base it on the example of how NuBoCo helps AirCo to succeed on page 45).
- For your chosen customer, make a list of *everyone who benefits* from your contribution and *how they benefit.*
- Now describe each of these benefits in terms of the Big Five (response, service, time, quality and price). This task is really important, because from now on you need to look at *exactly* how you create value for customers (like NuBoCo created value for AirCo).

- There is one final but important task for this chapter: you need to decide on a disciplined record-keeping process that will allow you to talk to customers about their business – and about what they value and will pay for. As stated on page 47, it is vital that you get out into the market and start talking to it – on a structured, regular basis.

All this knowledge will be essential for Chapter 4, as you get to grips with using the Big Five to motivate buying that creates profitable sales.

4

Working with buying motivators

BOOSTING SALES AND MARGINS –
HOW TO MOTIVATE YOUR MARKET TO BUY

Coming up in this chapter:
- How to motivate buying: a structured, disciplined approach
  - Introducing the value analysis process
  - How the value analysis process works
- Getting the process started: analysing the value you offer
  - Step 1: Value mining – What are you *really* selling?
  - Who needs to be part of the value mining process?
  - What results can you expect from value mining?
- Continuing the value analysis process
  - Step 2: Value mapping – What are your customers *really* buying?
  - Who needs to be part of the value mapping process?
  - What results can you expect from value mapping?
- Completing the value analysis process
  - Step 3: Value matching – How are you delivering what customers value?
  - Who needs to be part of the value matching process?
  - What results can you expect from value matching?
  - How value works in the real world: measuring the value gap
  - They're not buying! What's gone wrong?!

HOW TO MOTIVATE BUYING:
A STRUCTURED, DISCIPLINED APPROACH

Introducing the value analysis process

In Chapter 3 (B2B's Big Five buying motivators), we looked at how B2B buying is entirely driven by the five factors of value: response, service, time, quality and price.

You saw that value can be defined rather than treated as something vague and intangible. A key point is that customers are only willing to pay for things that contribute to their success. If they can't see how your products and services do that, they won't pay the price you want for them. This *always* leads to problems around price. Customers need to see the value in what you're selling in order for you to sell. Customers need to understand all the reasons why your price is the right price for them.

CUSTOMERS NEED TO UNDERSTAND
ALL THE REASONS WHY YOUR PRICE
IS THE RIGHT PRICE FOR THEM

Think for a moment about all the organisations you know that talk about creating and adding value for customers. Do those organisations really know what they mean? And much more importantly: do their customers know?

You need to cut through your brochure-speak and present customers with what they will pay for. To do this, you need to *analyse* how you create the value that motivates your customers to buy.

This brings us to a process called *value analysis*.

How the value analysis process works

Higher value, adding value, creating value, providing value: What does all of this *really* mean? Value analysis enables you to translate the value of what you are selling into the language of what customers are buying.

Its purpose is to motivate B2B buying. Here is a short step-by-step summary of how it works.

VALUE ANALYSIS TRANSLATES WHAT YOU ARE SELLING INTO THE LANGUAGE OF WHAT CUSTOMERS ARE BUYING

Step 1: Value mining – What are you really selling?

In this first step you will analyse your products, services and processes in terms of the Big Five buying motivators. It is called 'value mining' because it digs deeply into exactly what it is that you're selling and how you work with your customers. It identifies and describes the value that you think your products and services *offer* your customers.

Step 2: Value mapping – What are your customers really buying?

The next step involves a similar analysis of everything that motivates your customers to buy from you. This time, you aren't looking at your products and services internally; you'll be looking from the outside, by talking to customers and audiences in the overall market. We looked at this in Chapter 1 (The big, big market). Here you'll be 'mapping' how your overall market thinks you *create* value in terms of the Big Five buying motivators.

Step 3: Value matching –
How are you delivering what customers value?

This last step addresses every business's nightmare scenario: They're not buying! What's gone wrong?! In this part of the process, you will *compare* what you're selling to the value customers are buying.

This third step highlights the changes you may be required to make to ensure that there's an exact match between what you say you are selling and what really motivates your customers to buy from you. This is why step 3 is called 'value matching'.

That's value analysis: three straightforward steps in a structured process that turns vague, intangible notions of value into commercially relevant facts. Let's look at each step in more detail now.

GETTING THE PROCESS STARTED: ANALYSING THE VALUE YOU OFFER

Step 1: Value mining – What are you *really* selling?

Value mining analyses the value that your products, services and processes offer. It's an *internally focused exercise* that enables you to begin the process of *describing your products, services and processes* in terms of the Big Five buying motivators. So let's get started:

1. Choose a product or service.
2. Use a simple table like the one shown in the example at the end of this chapter to compile a list that describes how you think your chosen product or service performs according to each definition for all Big Five factors of value.

   Here are some questions that might help you create your descriptions for the *response* factor:

   - How do you identify your customers' requirements? Explain in detail how this happens for your chosen product or service.
   - How does your chosen product or service meet these requirements? Describe fully what your customers achieve with the chosen product or service.
   - Describe in detail how you meet customers' expectations – how do you address issues to ensure that you consistently deliver the outcomes that customers expect from the chosen product or service?

3. How do you think your performance compares with that of your competitors? For each entry on your value mining list, give yourself a ranking from 1 to 5 (from 1 for very poor to 5 for very good).

What value do you think you are offering in terms of B2B's Big Five buying motivators with this particular product or service? The value mining part of the analysis process will tell you.

Who needs to be part of the value mining process?

Obviously, your marketing team will be part of the process. But in addition to them, it's clearly a good idea to involve your sales team right from the start.

Once you've built a list of statements that describe how you create value for *each* value factor, you will need to broaden the process by getting opinions from other key functions such as finance, technical, production and distribution. How do they all think the company creates value in terms of the Big Five value factors? Add their answers to your value mining list. You might be surprised at the insights your colleagues provide – particularly those who deal with customers regularly. They often know things about your business that they'd perhaps rather not tell you, and that you'd prefer not to hear. And they often know things about your business that might be a surprise to you – and not necessarily of the pleasant kind!

What results can you expect from value mining?

Value mining is not only an enlightening process; it is part of an in-depth analysis that uncovers the *truth* about why your products and services matter to customers. It reveals the commercial realities of *how* your company makes a positive contribution to your customers' success. Value mining enables you to begin defining the real reasons why the market should buy from you.

VALUE MINING HELPS YOU DEFINE THE REAL REASONS WHY THE MARKET SHOULD BUY FROM YOU

It will also bring you one step closer towards creating marketing messages that accurately address the Big Five buying motivators in your B2B environment.

However, value mining is only the first step in the value analysis process.

Because it is internally focused, value mining only deals with how you – and the rest of your company – perceive and describe the value your products and services offer your customers. It will reveal some home truths about your products and services. Some will be great; some will be not so great.

The next step, value mapping, is externally focused and reveals what the market and your customers are *really* buying.

It analyses what *they* value – and what they're willing to pay for.

VALUE MINING WILL REVEAL
SOME HOME TRUTHS – SOME GREAT;
SOME NOT SO GREAT

CONTINUING THE VALUE ANALYSIS PROCESS

During the value mining exercise, you looked at your company and its products internally to describe the value your products and services offer your customers. But enough navel-gazing: you now need to move on to the second step in the process and look outside your business – at what customers value.

Step 2: Value mapping – What are your customers *really* buying?

In terms of the actual analysis, value mapping is similar to value mining, but this time you're looking at what *motivates* your customers to buy. So, let's start in much the same way:

1. Choose the same product or service that you analysed in the value mining process.

2. Use a chart similar to the one in the example at the end of this section to compile a list that describes how customers regard the chosen product or service according to each definition for all of the Big Five factors of value. To help you get started, here are some typical questions you might ask your customers to describe the *quality* of your products.

- Why is the quality of our products and services significant? What positive contribution does quality make to your business?
- Which elements of your business benefit from this quality? How do they benefit?
- What features of the product or service are most important to the success of your business?
- Are there features of our products and services that are *not* important to your company?
- What features do you *wish* were included? What difference would this make to the success of your company?

You can now determine how your customers rate your performance in comparison to that of your competitors in terms of *quality*. Repeat the process for each of the Big Five on your value mapping list, and then give a ranking from 1 to 5 (from 1 for very poor to 5 for very good). How does the value you provide compare to that of your competitors? Value mapping will tell you.

HOW DOES THE VALUE YOU PROVIDE COMPARE TO THAT OF YOUR COMPETITORS? VALUE MAPPING WILL TELL YOU

Who needs to be part of the value mapping process?

Quite clearly, your customers need to be part of the process. This might create a little problem: if you're a marketer, how many of your customers have you met in order to discuss business?

A large part of B2B marketing takes place in an office and behind closed doors. In fact, it often takes place in a proverbial ivory tower that has little, if any, business contact with customers. You might have met some of your customers at a golf day or a seminar, or at a conference or a trade show. You probably talked about the weather, news, sport and the economy. But how much do you know about their business and the challenges they face? How much real *business* have you talked with customers?

I can hear you say: Ah, but surely that's what the sales team does. Yes, they may well do. But that's not the point. *You* also need to be talking to customers about how your products and services contribute to their success. And the value mapping process enables you to discover *all* the ways you do that.

However, you should not do so in isolation. It is very important to involve senior salespeople right from the start.

It's also important to be talking to all the right people within your customers' operations. You need to discover *who* benefits from the positive contributions created by your products and services – and *how* they benefit.

What results can you expect from value mapping?

Value mapping will give you an accurate understanding of what your customers *value* – and what they don't value – about your products and services. It will describe the reasons *why* they buy, based on the Big Five buying motivators.

Once you know what makes your customers buy, your marketing activities can be focused on one target: to motivate buying that leads to profitable sales.

You may well be surprised at what your customers value. In fact, what you're selling may not match what they're really looking to buy.

That's what the next section is all about: value *matching*.

A LARGE PART OF B2B MARKETING HAPPENS IN ISOLATION. THE VALUE MAPPING PROCESS ENCOURAGES MARKETERS TO TALK BUSINESS WITH CUSTOMERS

COMPLETING THE VALUE ANALYSIS PROCESS

Step 3: Value matching –
How are you delivering what customers value?

The first part of value matching is really easy: simply compare the results of your value mining and value mapping analyses.

As you make this comparison you may well be surprised by the differences between the results. In fact, you may be very surprised ...

Actually, it's really unlikely that there will be an exact match between what you think you're selling and what customers are really buying.

What the comparison will show you is the difference between how you rate your Big Five performance and how your customers rate it.

That brings us to the second part of value matching. This part needs a little more thought, as you will begin to *measure* the areas in which your customers say you do create value and where you don't.

- During the value mining exercise, you described the value you think your company offers customers. We'll call those results '*perceived* value'.
- The results from your value mapping describe the value that customers think they get from you. We'll call that '*received* value'.

When you think about it, *received* value is the one that really matters, because it measures the value that you are really creating for customers.

WHAT ASPECTS OF YOUR PRODUCTS AND SERVICES CREATE VALUE? THE VALUE MATCHING PROCESS WILL TELL YOU

Your customers should be crystal clear about how you create value. But all too often, it isn't clear at all.

Let's go back to NuBoCo, the nuts-and-bolts manufacturer we talked about in Chapter 3. We saw that NuBoCo is providing its market with far more than nuts and bolts. They are providing a range of named services – for their product development programme, accredited dealers and certified products – all of which *create* value for their customers.

The people at NuBoCo know and appreciate how these different services contribute to their customers' successes. And because they choose to buy these services, their customers know it too.

The question here is: Do *your* customers know exactly what they are buying from you?

Who needs to be part of the value matching process?

Besides your sales team, you should involve everyone who is responsible for areas where there were differences between your value mining and value mapping analyses.

For example, if *quality* is not meeting customers' expectations, then you probably need to get input from manufacturing or your suppliers.

What results can you expect from value matching?

First of all, you can expect a clear insight into what is – and isn't – motivating customers to buy from you. That's the easy part.

The hard part is to decide what needs to change in order to create the right value for the right customers – and then to implement those changes.

This part may require a lot of collaboration between different functions within your organisation. If you get this right, you will be offering a range of products and services that are pretty much *irresistible*. It will give you an accurate road map for generating sales, building market share and protecting margins.

You will get a clear insight into what motivates customers to buy from you – and what doesn't.

How value works in the real world: measuring the value gap

The simple diagram below shows you some typical areas of over-delivery and under-delivery in relation to the Big Five buying motivators. It shows in which areas a customer thinks you are going over the top and in which areas he thinks you're not coming to the party.

The customer in this example is saying that part of your price offers no value – and why do you expect them to pay for it? This is a big problem, and it is called the 'value gap'.

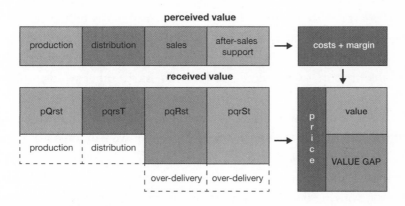

Perceived value vs. received value

The diagram shows an example of over- and under-delivery in different areas:

- The customer thinks that you are under-delivering in terms of production. In particular, they are saying that you are not delivering value in terms of the *quality* of your products, and that's why Q is capitalised.

- They also think that you aren't performing in terms of distribution and delivery. T (for *time*) is the main problem here – it seems it's taking too long to get hold of your products or too long for your services to be fulfilled.
- The customer also thinks you are doing far too much in other areas that are of little or no value to him – in this case, your sales efforts and your after-sales support. They might think that you are spending too much time fussing about whether they're okay and constantly sending sales reps and support staff around to check if they need anything. They don't see any value in your doing so.
- What they *do* need is faster fulfilment of services, faster delivery and higher product quality.

They're not buying! What's gone wrong?!

It should be clear from the right-hand column in the diagram that this is where the wheels start coming off. The customer is telling you that there is value in what he is buying from you – but not in everything.

The customer is saying that he does not want to pay for things that don't contribute to the success of his business. In other words, *he does not want to pay for things that don't create value.*

We've now discovered how to identify the value that motivates customers to buy – from you. In the next chapter, we will look at how to use this knowledge within your marketing. You will take everything you now know about your overall market and the Big Five value factors that motivate buying decisions and turn all of this information into *content* for your marketing.

DIRECTIONS TO RESULTS

Although there's quite a lot to do here, it's work with a vital purpose: it will tell you exactly how to match what you're selling to what customers are really motivated to buy. If you follow these directions, you'll be rocketing down the fast lane towards creating profitable sales.

Directions to results for Chapter 4 will show you:
- *how to describe all the ways in which you create value that motivates customers and prospects to buy from you*
- *how to overcome the price barrier by demonstrating why the value you create makes your price the right price.*

Follow these steps to get into the fast lane:
- Choose one product or service and one customer that currently buys it.
- Now complete each of the three steps of the value analysis process: value mining, value mapping and value matching (see page 55). Use the sample value analysis chart provided to help you do this.
- Once you've done this, you can start defining the value gap for your chosen customer: Where do they think you're under-delivering and over-delivering?
- What price-related problems are caused by the value gap? Are these problems caused by response, service, time or quality? Ask your colleagues in sales and support where they think the problems lie.
- Finally, decide what needs to be done to sort them out – and who needs to do it.

Sample value analysis chart

Here is an example of a simple value analysis chart. For the value mining exercise, list how you think your chosen product or service meets the definitions for each of the Big Five buying motivators.

RESPONSE
• Continual dialogue with customers; listening systematically to how you can build their success • Identifying and meeting your customers' changing needs • Solving problems and delivering solutions speedily
1
2
3
4

SERVICE
• Accessibility; an open and reassuring organisation • Clear information on products, services, processes and project status • Proactive and innovative service
1
2
3
4

TIME
• Competitive lead times • Dependable • Consistent delivery format
1
2
3
4

QUALITY
• Consistent products, services and processes • Meeting the brief or specifications reliably; providing fit-for-purpose products • Achieving the customer's goals
1
2
3
4

PRICE
• Clear • Competitive • Structured • Rational
1
2
3
4

5

Content is king!

WELCOME TO THE BRAND NEW,
AGE-OLD WORLD OF CONTENT MARKETING

Coming up in this chapter:
- Content marketing: What is it?
  - Big buzz, big results
  - Content and the B2B buying cycle
  - Content marketing's one goal: building buyer confidence
- Content marketing: how to do it
  - The right content, at the right time: getting in step with the buying cycle
  - Creating a content map: defining what to say
  - Inspiring contact, capturing contacts: managing calls-to-action
- What have you got to say for yourself? Creating content that motivates buying
  - Core brand messages: foundations for content that motivates buying
  - Tell the truth – be credible
  - Keep up with the times – stay relevant
- The three key Cs of content: concentrated, convincing, connected

CONTENT MARKETING: WHAT IS IT?

Big buzz, big results

Content marketing – or CM – is a pretty hot topic in B2B right now. This is hardly surprising, because what you say to the market is just as important now as it was before the world went digital and B2B marketers had to rely mainly on print advertising, PR, direct post, trade events and brochures.

In Chapter 2 (Things *are* what they used to be), we looked at the famous 1958 advert from McGraw-Hill known as 'The Man in the Chair' and found that over fifty years later, the Man is still asking the same big, basic questions:

- Who are you?
- What do you do?
- Why do you matter – to ME?

Those are *buyers'* questions. Buyers are still asking how you will contribute to their success. And *buyers* are what your answers should be all about, as said in Chapter 2.

But what about *content*? What does content mean? Content is a mix of design and copy that delivers answers to these three questions. And it has always been the cornerstone of B2B marketing.

Today, the purpose of content is still the same: to generate sales, protect margins and build market share – or at least, it *should* be. But quite clearly it hasn't been. And that's highlighted by a lot of so-called 'expert' talk about CM.

Most of this nonsense talk argues that 'traditional' B2B marketing has been based on self-centred brochure-speak about how world-leading and absolutely fabulous your company and your products are. In contrast – so the argument goes – CM is about focusing on customers and providing them with the information *they* want. This is a bit like claiming credit for reinventing the wheel.

Content marketing isn't a new idea that is somehow changing B2B's basic rules – the rules are still the same. Rather, CM is driven by the opportunities for communication that digital has created, and it has emerged as a *consequence* of advances in technology.

Marketers didn't develop web technology or smartphones. They didn't say: 'We need new ways to communicate with our market, so let's have a workshop and brainstorm how to invent email and webinars.'

So, *what* you need to say to the market hasn't changed. But the *ways* in which you can say it certainly have: today we have PDFs, video, social media, webinars, emails, online user groups and forums, slide-shares, ebooks and websites.

None of this existed back in '58!

CONTENT MARKETING COMBINES DIGITAL WITH TRADITIONAL, BUT B2B'S BASIC RULES STILL APPLY

Content marketing is all about communications that focus on the needs of the overall market and customers.

As a definition, this may sound a bit simplistic. But the word 'communicate' comes from the Latin for 'sharing'. And that's exactly what CM does: it shares your information with the overall market and customers.

The implication of sharing is that it works in two ways: *If your communication is relevant and credible, then the market will want to talk to you.*

Although CM certainly capitalises on digital channels by extending *how* you communicate, CM does not mean excluding print advertising, PR, trade events and brochures from your overall communications strategy.

As in 1958, today's B2B buyers still read magazines, journals and newspapers. They still attend live events and they still like hard-copy brochures for all the relevant facts and figures. So all that's really changed is that marketers now have a new set of communication channels. But *what* they still need to be saying via those channels hasn't changed.

If the buzz around CM encourages marketers to get back to B2B's basic rules to focus on telling their market what it needs to hear – in order to motivate *buying* – then content marketing is a good thing.

If you understand and apply the basic rules, your marketing will do its job. It will generate sales, protect margins and build market share.

Content and the B2B buying cycle

B2B buying certainly doesn't happen on a sudden impulse: 'Buddy, let's buy an earthmover.' 'Yeah, neat! Let's do it!' It typically includes six phases, starting with identifying a need and ending with buying whatever item addresses that need. Here is an overview of the six phases of the B2B buying cycle.

Start		**B2B buying cycle**			Finish
Phase 1	**Phase 2**	**Phase 3**	**Phase 4**	**Phase 5**	**Phase 6**
Identifying needs	Setting criteria	Specific research	Evaluation and testing	Selecting suppliers and negotiating	Buying and implementing

In Chapter 2 (Things *are* what they used to be), we looked at how the information superhighway enables the overall market to form opinions about your company and your products and services long before contacting you directly.

Increasingly, your market *expects* to complete phases 1, 2 and 3 on its own – *before* the sales cycle even starts. The market is selling to itself and shortening the sales cycle.

THE MARKET IS SELLING TO ITSELF
AND SHORTENING THE SALES CYCLE

It is quite scary if your products and services don't feature in the minds of customers and prospects during the first three phases of the cycle. If buyers are only asking you 'How much?', they already know what they're looking for. They're already halfway through the cycle and have pretty much decided where they're going and who's going with them.

Self-educated B2B buyers are self-sold buyers. They may be so far advanced in the cycle that their first contact with your company is just to ask for a price.

SELF-EDUCATED B2B BUYERS
ARE SELF-SOLD BUYERS

Content marketing's one goal: building buyer confidence

Content marketing has one goal: to generate sales-creating trust. How do you go about doing this? As a first step, take a careful look at the six phases of the buying cycle: you can use the buying cycle's six phases as a guide to construct a 'content map' that can guarantee that you will provide your prospective customers with the right content at the right time.

The content map on page 75 shows the type of content that builds buyers' confidence in you as they move through the cycle. And it shows *when* this content is needed. The point is that the type of content that's needed remains constant and has been the same since the year dot – whether or not people are using the internet to access the content and sell to themselves. What *has* changed is behaviour in the cycle – internet-enabled buyers no longer have to start the cycle through direct contact with vendors.

The B2B content map is a guide for defining marketing content that provides the right information at the right time. It is not a rigid rule book that segments your content into prison cells. Some content flows through more than one phase, particularly during the first three phases.

Your content should build buyers' confidence as they progress through each phase of the buying cycle. It should generate sales-creating trust.

Now you need to think about how to *create* content for each phase in the buying cycle.

As you begin to consider the type of content you need, it's important to have a clear objective in mind: content must motivate buying. In the words of the famous management consultant Peter Drucker:

The aim of marketing is to make selling unnecessary.

Creating content that motivates buying – and therefore makes selling unnecessary – is what we're going to look at in the next section of this chapter. B2B buyers need confidence that they're making the right decisions. Confidence matters because it generates demand. And demand generates sales.

CONFIDENCE MATTERS BECAUSE IT GENERATES DEMAND. AND DEMAND GENERATES SALES

Start	B2B content map: building sales-creating trust				Finish
Phase 1	**Phase 2**	**Phase 3**	**Phase 4**	**Phase 5**	**Phase 6**
Identifying needs	Setting criteria	Specific research	Evaluation and testing	Selecting suppliers and negotiating	Buying and implementing
Buyers need:	Buyers need:	Buyers need:	Buyers need:	Buyers need:	Buyers need:
INSIGHT	**KNOWLEDGE**	**FACTS**	**EVIDENCE**	**REINFORCEMENT**	**FULFILMENT**
Motivating change: business needs, trend and product analysis, industry objectives	**Buyer checklists:** industry specific, glossary, knowledge test, FAQs	**Operational:** product guides, technical data, fact sheets, trial results	**For products:** proof-of-concept structures, costs and requirements	**Company info:** financials, future stability, plans	Contracts, terms, pricing models, legal, process reporting and escalation, problem solving
Business case: opinion articles, buying trends, challenges, future direction	**Feature and benefits analysis:** attainable benefits, life cycles, best practices	**Business case:** analyst reports, case studies, ownership costs	**For services:** testimonials, case studies, user groups, peer-to-peer	**Case studies:** processes, SLAs and support, ROI, after-sales outcomes, progress monitoring, account management, project management	
Company info: achievements, objectives, visions of the future	**Case studies:** meeting criteria, ROI and budgets, managing projects	Price guides	**Company info:** skills, people, processes	Quotes, terms and proposals	
	Legal and standards compliance	**Calls-to-action:** offers, contact requests, diarise, share, downloads, mailing new content, sign-up	**Documented:** trial criteria and outcomes, technical reporting		
	Needs analysis: processes and templates	**Placement and distribution:** mail and SEO, blogs, user groups, links website, social	Pricing and proposals		
		Contact and lead management	**Comparative:** matrix analysis and SWOT		

The B2B content map: building sales-creating trust

CONTENT MARKETING: HOW TO DO IT

What you say in advertising is more important than how you say it. — David Ogilvy

A lot of the buzz around CM deals with the mechanics of providing content in formats that suit delivery across different channels. Usually the emphasis is on digital. This buzz is mostly about *packaging*. It focuses on the wrapping paper and the dinky little box in which your content comes. In fact, the *content* of your content is rarely mentioned.

Of course, *what* you need to say – what's in the box – is way more important than *how* you say it.

If the 'packagistes' do mention *what* you need to be saying, it's often no more useful than suggesting you should be providing 'quality content', 'exceptional content', 'thought-leading content', 'amazing content', 'compelling content' and 'more content' – all meaningless brochurespeak. But:

B2B buyers aren't motivated to buy things because they like the box. It's the content in the box that motivates buying.

So how to create *motivating* content is what we're going to look at now.

The right content, at the right time: getting in step with the buying cycle

The B2B buying cycle starts with customers identifying a business need and ends with them buying what's necessary to meet that need according to a set of criteria.

Those criteria are *always* based on B2B's Big Five buying motivators: response, service, time, quality and price.

When you think carefully about this, you may notice that buyers are always asking questions that relate directly to the Big Five: 'What do we need, why do we need it, what's available, who understands it, who sells it, what are they like, how does it work, when can we have it?' And: 'What will it all cost?'

As consumers, we usually don't ask all those questions, because our needs are a lot simpler. We quickly identify them: 'There's no toothpaste';

'We need petrol'; 'I've got nothing to wear!' And we buy our 'solutions' from suppliers we already know and trust. We go straight from phase 1 to phase 6, although there might be a bit of phase 5 on the way to selecting where we buy it, and possibly a bit of haggling.

B2B buying is very different. B2B buyers need confidence-building content that's relevant to where they are in the buying cycle – content that will motivate them to move to the next phase. So don't put the cart in front of the horse: deciding on *what* you say comes before *how* you say it. (We'll be looking at how to deliver your content – and make sure it reaches the right people – in Chapter 7.)

Creating a content map: defining what to say

During phases 1, 2 and 3, customers build confidence in their decision-making process through three types of information: insight, knowledge and facts (look at the first three columns of the B2B content map diagram).

What they're not looking for is that dreadful, over-worked expression of 'thought leadership'. It's not a dreadful expression because it's over-worked. It's dreadful because it oozes notions that are pretentious, self-centred and arrogant: it suggests you know more about your customers' business than they do. (How dare you!)

Instead, your content should focus on things that it *is* your business to know about: how your products, services and processes create value for your customers.

If your content is relevant and credible, customers will want to talk to you.

**IF YOUR CONTENT IS RELEVANT
AND CREDIBLE, CUSTOMERS
WILL WANT TO TALK TO YOU**

Phase 1: Identifying needs

Type of content that buyers need: Insight

In phase 1 (shown as the first column of the B2B content map diagram), customers are thinking about improving their enterprise. Your content should emphasise that you know your market, the challenges it is facing and how to meet those challenges.

This means that you may need to *motivate change.*

You can do this by highlighting how you can help customers respond positively to what is happening around them.

If you demonstrate insight into your customers' needs and how these needs are changing, you show that you're in tune with your market's challenges.

And your market will want to listen to you.

Insight says that you *understand* the challenges.

Phase 2: Setting criteria

Type of content that buyers need: Knowledge

Phase 2 content should show that you know that customers' resources are finite and that they operate within a set of guidelines or criteria.

For example, budgets dictate that there's only a set amount of money to meet challenges (and to buy and use your products and services). Human resources and skills sets also have limits. So do other criteria, such as office or factory space and geographical locations.

An understanding of these enables you to demonstrate knowledge of *how* your products and services will make a practical contribution to your customers' success.

It also demonstrates that you want to help customers make objective and rational assessments of how they can advance their enterprise.

A willingness to share relevant and credible knowledge motivates customers to listen and ask for more.

Phase 3: Specific research

Type of content that buyers need: Facts

The *insight* and *knowledge* you displayed in phases 1 and 2 now need to be complemented in phase 3 by relevant, operational *facts*. Insight and knowledge demonstrate that you understand *how to solve* customers' challenges. Facts say you *can solve them.*

Content for phase 3 is about how stuff works – how your company works and how your products and services will work to build your customers' success.

It should be current, accurate, clear and sufficiently comprehensive to answer the questions that are relevant at this point in the cycle. Factual content should not need loads of additional explanation or raise more questions than it answers.

An important part of phase 3 is calls-to-action or CTAs. While they should feature in phases 1 and 2, *easy access* to all content via simple CTAs is what motivates prospective clients to pay you more attention.

CTAs are critical in phase 3, because buyers now want very specific information. And you certainly want to capture more than their attention; you want to know *who they are.*

In phase 3, you're being eyeballed by serious buyers. These people probably have money to spend. That's why this is a good time to look at CTAs.

KNOWLEDGE SHOWS THAT YOU UNDERSTAND HOW TO SOLVE CUSTOMERS' CHALLENGES. FACTS SHOW YOU CAN SOLVE THEM

Inspiring contact, capturing contacts: managing calls-to-action

In phase 3, the opportunity to capture contacts is greater than it was earlier in the cycle. Some of your phase 1 and 2 content might be so good that you think it deserves an online sign-up to access it. But perhaps it's better to include sign-up as an option *within* the content you are providing: 'Interested? Why not sign up for more through our newsletter?'

When you create CTAs, think like your customers do. Imagine that you're part of a team that has been tasked with buying products and services similar to yours. Once you've reached phase 3 of the buying cycle, you want practical information. You might join a user group, accept a special trial offer, or attend a product focus day, seminar, trade show or conference.

In phases 1 and 2, if people think they need to talk to your company, they'll call. If they don't, they won't. Let them choose.

During these two phases, would you consider registering on a website merely in order to be able to download PDFs of media coverage or a couple of product sheets? Especially if you don't want a sales call? You might sign up for a case study on solving typical challenges within your industry (although, then again, you might not).

The issue with including CTAs in the first two phases is this: do you want people to read your content and be inspired to want more, or do you want to lose their interest by forcing them to provide their contact details?

What you really want is that your phase 1 and 2 content will *inspire* them to move to phase 3.

Before we continue, it will be helpful to do some navel-gazing about the *expectations* you created in the first three phases.

Why? Because you need to be certain that your content from the first three phases will stand the test of moving through the next three.

Customers want the information from phases 1, 2 and 3 – and the confidence it builds – to be reinforced from this point onwards.

You need to be sure that your company and its products and services can *walk the talk*, as prospective buyers move into phase 4.

INSPIRE PEOPLE TO READ YOUR CONTENT AND WANT MORE. DON'T PUSH THEM AWAY BY FORCING THEM TO PROVIDE THEIR DETAILS TOO SOON

Phase 4: Evaluation and testing

Type of content that buyers need: Evidence

Because customers today move through phases 1 to 3 mostly on their own, this is where the modern B2B sales cycle might typically start. It is here that the nitty-gritty of the *performance* of your products and services starts.

Buyers need to be convinced that everything you offer will work in their environment, and that all the expectations you created during phases 1 to 3 will be fulfilled. Or not.

It's at this point that you will be seen as credible. Or not.

Because this is where buyers' confidence in you will be put to the test.

It's also the point at which buyers need clarity – documented clarity – on the processes that govern how you manage product tests or conduct a proof-of-concept.

Typical questions in this phase are:
- What are the cost implications?
- How long will a test last?
- What agreed results are critical to its success?
- What resources are typically required?
- What are the lead times to initiate the test?

All the information to answer these questions needs to be clear, current and readily available.

When it comes to evaluations, product testing is typically more straightforward than testing a service or a process: you can test-drive an 18-wheeler – but can you test the dealer's service department?

Buyers want to assess the performance of your services and processes, so you need to provide evidence. This evidence might include customer testimonials and site visits, independent research and test reports, best-practice guides based on customer experiences, case studies and user-group findings.

Your phase 4 content also needs to be *relevant* to your customer's business and the challenges that each element of their business is facing.

EVIDENCE PROVES YOU CAN WALK THE TALK

Phase 5: Selecting suppliers and negotiating
Type of content that buyers need: Reinforcement
Phase 5 is the point at which buyers select potential suppliers and start talking turkey. The type of information they want at this point in the buying cycle is very specific indeed. They don't want information on industry and product trends, because they already have that.

They certainly don't want to hear about how you can help them identify their needs – they've already covered all that way back in phase 1.

What they want are assurances that *reinforce* their confidence that your company will meet the expectations you have created during the previous phases. They're not interested in those assurances before they reach phase 5. If you offer these earlier, this will sound like 'Ain't we fab!' self-promotion on your part – and it won't be listened to or treated as credible.

Phase 6: Buying and implementing
Type of content that buyers need: Fulfilment
This is where it's at, so no surprises here, please! If your buyers have reached this point, it means they have had no surprises in phases 4 or

5 either. So it is best not to create any now. You certainly don't want any small print and dodgy exception clauses to bite the hand that's about to feed you.

> *The large print giveth and the small print taketh away.*
> – Tom Waits, from the song 'Step Right Up'

But remember that content can't create confidence if nobody sees it.

Content has to be visible.

So you need to make sure that you reach *all* the audiences in your sphere of influence. Choosing the channels that will reach them is covered in Chapter 7 (Extra special delivery).

Right now, you still need to look at how you translate what you are saying into the language that motivates buying. And that's discussed next in this chapter.

AVOID SMALL PRINT AND DODGY EXCEPTION CLAUSES THAT BITE THE HAND THAT'S ABOUT TO FEED YOU

WHAT HAVE YOU GOT TO SAY FOR YOURSELF?
CREATING CONTENT THAT MOTIVATES BUYING

In this chapter so far, we have been looking at the type of things you need to say to your market, and when you need to be saying them.

You now need to get more specific and look at *precisely what* you should be saying to your customers to motivate buying.

Some repetition might help here: before you can decide *how* you want to say something, you first need to know *what* you want to say.

That's not a big problem. In Chapter 4 (Working with buying motivators), you analysed what motivates customers to buy from you. So as far as specific content goes, you already know *what* you want to say because you have all the raw, fact-based information about how you create value and contribute to your customers' success.

You can now use this priceless information to create something we call 'core brand messages' or CBMs (jargony acronyms can sometimes be useful).

CBMs are short 'headlines' that grab attention and generate interest in what you say to each audience in your overall B2B market.

Core brand messages: foundations for content that motivates buying

If you want your core brand messages, or CBMs, to build the confidence that motivates buying, they have to tell customers *how* you deliver on the Big Five buying motivators: response, service, time, quality and price.

So you have to translate what you are selling into the language of the Big Five.

Here's an example of how this 'translation' works in relation to quality. In 'Marketing in the B2B environment', we looked at how a manufacturer of earthmovers might communicate how reliability provides different benefits for different people within its customer base.

In terms of the Big Five, reliability relates to quality. But the manufacturer can't buy a box of reliability. It's a *benefit* created by a variety of technical features incorporated within the earthmover.

Reliability is a result of the design, engineering and consequent performance of things like the earthmover's engine, suspension, transmission and hydraulics, as well as adherence to standards that govern component testing, manufacturing processes and overall build quality.

This is what your market wants and needs to know. So your CBMs about quality must be attention-grabbing headlines that tell the market how all those features *translate* into fabulous reliability.

TRANSLATE WHAT YOU ARE REALLY SELLING INTO THE LANGUAGE OF WHAT THE MARKET IS REALLY BUYING

Tell the truth – be credible

To build confidence and motivate buying, you have to tell the truth. But the truth needs to be well told, or it might not attract any attention and won't generate credibility.

'Our earthmovers are the very best!' might be true, but is it credible?

The notion of the selling power of truth is not new. The slogan 'Truth well told' was introduced by Harrison King McCann back in 1912 at the launch of his New York advertising agency. Over a hundred years later it is still being used by one of the world's biggest advertising agencies, McCann Erickson.

- Credible content must be kept factual, as brief as possible and in a format that will be readily understood and familiar to your audience. Clever infographics may look great on the page, but make sure they are designed so that all your audiences will be comfortable with them and quickly understand them.

- Also, make sure that your content serves its purpose: it must build the confidence that motivates buying from *you*. Unless you work for a trade association, you aren't in the business of promoting anyone else's offering.

- Finally, make sure that it's well written: Is the meaning crystal clear? And is it straightforward and to the point?

Keep up with the times – stay relevant

Credibility needs to be combined with relevance. This may sound pretty obvious, but many B2B companies push the same messages at the same time to different people with different job functions in their sphere of influence.

Purely by coincidence, some of it will be relevant to some people. But it certainly won't be relevant to *all* the people who influence buying decisions.

Content needs to address the commercial, working interests of each audience in your sphere. Engineers want and need technical content, accountants want and need financial content.

If you want to stay relevant, you need an up-to-date understanding of what's happening in your market and the context in which customers are operating.

A straightforward example of context is the current recession: recessions breed caution, and right now, all around you, companies are holding back on spending. This is not simply because of budget constraints. Conservatism reigns.

A LACK OF CONFIDENCE IN THE ECONOMY HEIGHTENS THE AWARENESS OF RISK AND THIS CREATES BARRIERS TO SPENDING

Content must serve its purpose: to build the confidence that motivates buying. From *you*.

Uncertainty makes people nervous and corporate purse-strings tighten. So customers need to feel particularly secure in their purchasing decisions. They want to make really low-risk buying decisions coupled with clearly presented, tangible rewards.

So what should you be doing right now? You need to create content that is grounded in reassurances about issues such as low-risk, demonstrable ROI and cost savings.

But you still need to show how your products and services create opportunities for your customers to grow: to build *their* sales and protect *their* margins and market share.

Staying relevant is an ongoing process that needs to be in tune with your customers' environment and how it is changing.

We saw how that all works, and how it changes depending on circumstances, with King Richard and his horse back in Chapter 3.

THE THREE KEY Cs OF CONTENT: CONCENTRATED, CONVINCING, CONNECTED

You will need to focus very clearly on what you are aiming for when creating content. You can do this by using the three Cs of content. They're a quick and handy checklist to make sure your content is always heading in the right direction and consist of three words: concentrated, convincing and connected.

- *Concentrated*: your content has a single focus – to build sales-creating trust
- *Convincing*: your content is relevant and credible to each influencer
- *Connected*: your content motivates customers' buying decisions in your favour.

Since marketing is essentially about creating and managing positive perceptions of your company that reinforce your markets' confidence in your products and services, it's important to ensure *unity* in all your content.

Without unity, you risk diluting the credibility of your CBMs, allowing your audiences to form the wrong impressions about your brand.

That is why brands and branding are the focus of the next chapter.

DIRECTIONS TO RESULTS

Developing content that generates sales-creating trust is not a once-off exercise. But although it's an ongoing task that needs to maintain relevance, you do need to start by laying some solid foundations on which you can build your content.

Directions to results for Chapter 5 will show you:
- *how to create content that is relevant for each phase in the buying cycle and for each audience in your spheres of influence*
- *how to create credible, trusted content that will motivate the buying that creates profitable sales.*

Follow these steps to get into the fast lane:
- Start compiling a content map like the one on page 75. This will help you list the type of content you need for each phase in the buying cycle.
- The next step is to start populating your content map with content that is relevant and credible. On page 76 you'll find the guidance you need on how to create content that addresses the right issues at the right time.
- Define the core brand message (CBM) for each of your products and services. These are the short headlines that grab attention and generate interest in your content from each audience member in your market. CBMs were covered on page 84.
- Once you have done all this, do a quick 'relevance audit': Is your content currently relevant for its phase and for its target audience?
- Now run a credibility check on your content. Is it telling the truth? Is it presented in a professional and appropriate way for each of the audiences in your sphere? Will it be trusted?

- Think about your calls-to-action and be realistic about how you expect your audience to react to your content. Be clear about what action you want the audience to take and how you will respond when they take it.
- And, last but certainly not least, check that your content really does comply with the three Cs of content covered on page 87: Is it concentrated? Is it convincing? Is it connected?

How you reach the right people with your content is covered in Chapter 7 – once we've taken a critical look at the subjects of brands and branding in Chapter 6.

6

Brands and branding: B2B's profit-pumping heart

HOW BRANDS BUILD BUSINESS

Coming up in this chapter:
- Brands mean ownership
  - What is a brand and why does it matter?
  - What is branding and why does it matter?
  - What ownership *really* means
  - How brands build business
- Building confidence: the sole purpose of B2B branding
  - Expectation + experience = confidence
- What is *your* brand?
  - Your brand in the mirror: market reflections
  - Market reflections: you are what the market says you are
  - Market reflections: how they control sales, margins and market share
  - Are they really talking about us?
- Your company *is* the brand, so *be* the brand!
  - Brand unity: meeting expectations
- Creating your brand: 'idealized redesign'

BRANDS MEAN OWNERSHIP

What is a brand and why does it matter?

A brand is a visible mark of ownership. Burn your mark into a cow's backside and you create a sign that says you own that cow. The sign – the brand – represents ownership.

Ever since the earliest days of branding cattle, its purpose hasn't changed. It's still a visible mark of ownership.

A lot of marketing talk today is about brands, and not much of it still has to do with burning permanent marks on cows.

So there is not much talk about ownership.

This is strange.

It's strange because in B2B, your brand should be saying: we *own* this product or service and, most of all, we own the positive contributions it makes to our customers' success.

It should be saying: we own the outcomes that are produced by its characteristics. We own its reliability, its short lead times, its quality, its support, its maintenance, its competitive pricing and how we work with our customers on positive future developments.

A brand says that all of these things are ours: this is what we own. Therefore, this is what we represent.

The link between brand and ownership is critically important.

Here's an example: How many times have you remembered a fab ad but forgotten the brand? 'Great ad! It's clever, striking, sharp, funny, hard-hitting. Er, but what company was it again?' If there is no brand ownership, there's no point in advertising!

What you own isn't represented by your logo, its shape, its colours or its slogans. That's design and copywriting. It's not your brand.

Your brand is the sum of all the reasons why customers should buy from you. That's why your brand is commercially so important.

A brand is a visible mark that tells a story about ownership. It'll work to your advantage to keep this in mind as we look in more detail at B2B brands and branding.

YOUR BRAND IS THE SUM
OF ALL THE REASONS WHY
CUSTOMERS SHOULD BUY FROM YOU

What is branding and why does it matter?
Branding entails all the ways in which your brand comes alive.

It's *how* you put your brand to work.

Brands create *expectations*. Branding creates *experiences*.

BRANDS CREATE EXPECTATIONS.
BRANDING CREATES EXPERIENCES

Your branding should constantly reinforce the ways in which you are making positive contributions to your customers' success.

Through every experience that a customer has of your brand – from how your phones are answered, right through to after-sales service – branding is about how you demonstrate what your brand represents.

And branding matters. When a strong brand is applied strongly, the consequences are all good:

- Branding attracts new customers and sidelines the competition.
- Branding protects your margins and reinforces customer loyalty.
- Branding generates more sales and accelerates sales cycles.

There's nothing touchy-feely about branding. It has a real, commercial purpose: to create sales, protect margins and build market share.

We'll look at why and how it produces those results later in this chapter (see page 98).

But first we need to look at the commercial significance of the link between brands and ownership.

BRANDING HAS A COMMERCIAL PURPOSE: TO BUILD SALES AND PROTECT MARGINS

What ownership *really* means

Now that we've got the definitions of brand and branding sorted, let's go back and talk some more about cows.

Big John Rancher brands all his cattle with the letters BJR.

What does BJR mean to the different people – all the different audiences – who see that brand? What do they think it represents? Let's hear them out!

- *The cattle rustler*: 'Everyone knows that BJR will hunt you down and shoot you full of holes if you steal his cows. Let's move on. Quickly.'
- *The bulk beef buyer*: 'BJR breeds the best beef there is. He drives a hard bargain, but if you want to be wholesaling the best, BJR's your man.'
- *The bulk milk buyer*: 'BJR has the finest dairy herd around. It's the best milk money can buy. It makes us a small fortune.'
- *The hide buyer*: 'If you want hides that are all torn and scarred and cheap, don't waste your breath talking to BJR.'
- *The health inspector*: 'It's always a pleasure to give BJR's cattle a clean bill of health. He's the best rancher we know.'
- *The butcher*: 'We can't get enough of that BJR beef. It sells like hot cakes!'
- *The braai master*: 'If it says BJR on the box, it's great. There's no other steak like it. Mmm!'
- *The competition*: 'Damn that man! Let's switch to sheep.'

All of this from a simple sign – a brand. This brand tells a *big* story about ownership: BJR is a lot more than a burn mark on a cow's behind!

WHEN EVERYONE WHO INFLUENCES BUYING DECISIONS SEES YOUR BRAND, WHAT DO THEY THINK?

How brands build business

The fact that brands build and sustain business really is a no-brainer. For example, when it comes to cans of baked beans, there is only one brand for me. I'll go bean-less rather than buy another brand. But is the same true for a company buying a baked-bean canning plant? In other words, are brands and branding important in B2B?

The answer is that if your brand generates associations of trust, satisfaction and fulfilled expectations, then customers won't look anywhere else – they won't even consider another canning-plant supplier.

And the reason why they won't look anywhere else for that mega-bucks canning plant is that they are 100 per cent confident that their preferred supplier will meet their needs across each of the Big Five buying motivators.

BUYERS NEED 100 PER CENT CONFIDENCE THAT THEY'RE MAKING THE RIGHT DECISION

BUILDING CONFIDENCE: THE SOLE PURPOSE OF B2B BRANDING

Building and maintaining customers' confidence generates sales, protects margins and builds market share: confidence that your products and services will contribute to their success; confidence that buying from you will be consistent with past experiences or proposed deliverables.

The word 'confidence' just keeps cropping up. Confidence! Confidence! Confidence!

Why? In the previous chapter, we looked at the fact that there is a *direct* relationship between confidence and sales: confidence generates demand, and demand generates sales. Confidence is seriously important – which means that *branding* is also seriously important, because your branding should be focused on building buyers' confidence.

Expectation + experience = confidence

The level of confidence you create among B2B buyers is based entirely on your performance in terms of the Big Five buying motivators.

We looked at how your products and services should deliver on the Big Five in Chapter 4 (Working with buying motivators). However … simply because you *tell* the market how you deliver on the Big Five doesn't mean that you *are* delivering on them. You might be able to talk the talk, but can you walk the walk?

A key marketing function is to govern every interaction with the market. That's a challenge we'll look at in Chapter 8 (Marketing united).

If you don't meet the expectations you set, then you won't build confidence. There's a direct relationship between expectation, experience and the market's confidence in your brand. This diagram will show you how this works:

The relationship between expectations, experiences and confidence

If customers don't believe that you are delivering on the Big Five, they will start losing confidence. They lose trust in you because you promise big and deliver small. Big John Rancher would probably say: 'Those guys?! Big hat, no cattle.'

You will soon feel the consequences of low confidence: sales will fall, margins will fall and market share will fall – all because your company is not *being* the brand. Because your brand has no credibility. Like this:

'Your call is important to us. Please hold. For exceptionally large orders, press 1. Thank you. Please hold while we transfer you. Your call is important to us. We are now transferring your call to our Exceptionally Large Order Department. Please hold. Your call ...'

Not good. Not good at all. But before we get to the concept of brand unity we're going to step back and ask: What is *your* brand?

NEVER PROMISE BIG AND DELIVER SMALL

WHAT IS *YOUR* BRAND?

Your brand in the mirror: market reflections

Imagine you are holding your logo up to a mirror. It's a clever mirror because the image you see staring back is your personal *perception* of the company and what it represents.

When your CEO holds the logo up to this mirror, what image is reflected? Does the CEO see what you see? Is the same image reflected when your colleagues from production, customer support, finance, sales and distribution hold the logo up to the mirror?

Probably not. Typically, there will be as many different reflections as there are people looking in the mirror. And if that's the case, the result is confusion. All those different reflections create an image that is completely meaningless.

And that's a very real problem. Because, of course, this is a *real* mirror.

The mirror is your market and your customers. The reflection they see *is* your brand.

Market reflections: you are what the market says you are

Back in Chapter 1 (The big, big market), you looked at the sphere of influence and the multiple audiences that make up an overall B2B market.

When you completed the Directions to Results exercise at the end of that chapter, you listed all the various audiences in your sphere and defined how they influence buying decision makers. That's good, because you know *who* is looking in the mirror.

Whatever each audience sees in the mirror is a market reflection. And it is these market reflections – and only these – that *create* your brand.

Through your brand and branding, you must create unity in what the market sees.

It's this unity that controls your ability to generate sales, protect margins and build market share. Brands and the branding that drives them clearly matter.

In B2B, your brand is created entirely by the market. This is where your sales and margins come from.

IN B2B, YOUR BRAND IS CREATED ENTIRELY BY THE MARKET. WHAT THE MARKET THINKS IS ALL THAT MATTERS

Market reflections: how they control sales, margins and market share

What a company thinks of its brand is completely irrelevant in comparison to what the market thinks.

What the market sees reflected by your brand is all that matters.

If the market cannot clearly understand what your brand represents, then your brand might as well be symbolised by something equally meaningless. We've all seen plenty of meaningless logos. A red camel eating a blue banana may be beautiful, bright and vibrant. But what does it mean?

Customers become confused and uncertain if the image your brand reflects is unclear and inconsistent.

If there's no clear sense of what you *own* and no immediate sense of what your brand *represents*, customers are forced to figure it out by themselves and draw their own conclusions.

They set their own expectations and decide for themselves how much *confidence* they have in your company, your products and your services.

The loss of brand ownership and confidence in your brand has two damaging consequences. First, sales fall, margins get squeezed and market share drops. Secondly, your brand and your branding generate perceptions in the market that have no relation to what your company might *really* represent:

- 'I thought you guys would be way too expensive for us.'
- 'We just can't figure out what you guys can do for us.'
- 'I didn't realise you guys could give us all that.'
- 'What? You mean you understand how to handle this too?'
- 'I had no idea you could work with us internationally.'
- 'Oh yeah, I know those guys. They sell red bananas and blue camels. Er, don't they?'

SALES, MARGINS AND MARKET SHARE ARE CREATED BY ONE THING: HOW THE MARKET SEES YOU

Are they really talking about us?

Increasingly, market reflections – the perceptions created by your brand in the market – are what influence your ability to generate sales, build market share and protect margins.

This influence is increasing as more and more lanes get added to the information superhighway, and customers are increasingly able to find what they need to know about your company and your products and services on the internet without any direct contact with you.

You already know how all this works and understand the signifi-cance of self-sold buyers in the B2B buying cycle that we looked at in Chapter 2 (Things *are* what they used to be: B2B's basic rules).

This influence is growing: digital media have a major impact on market reflections. Social media sites actively encourage people to discuss and *share* their experiences about vendors and their products and services. This cuts both ways of course, as vendors are joining the discussions in an attempt to present their brand messages over more channels and interact more directly with each of their audiences. Digital media are making you more visible to everyone who influences buying decisions.

The more channels you use to communicate what your brand represents in order to motivate buying, the more the chances increase for your market reflection to become jumbled and meaningless.

It is now more important than ever to present a cohesive, confidence-boosting reflection of your brand.

- It must be visible, credible and relevant to each audience in your overall market.
- Your brand must create positive perceptions among all the different people who influence buying decisions.

DIGITAL MEDIA ARE MAKING YOU MORE VISIBLE TO EVERYONE WHO INFLUENCES BUYING DECISIONS

YOUR COMPANY *IS* THE BRAND, SO *BE* THE BRAND!

Brand management is most definitely *not* the business of designers and communications agencies. It simply isn't.

It's not that designers and agencies produce poor or inappropriate work. It's just that they have no *control* over how their clients build confidence by consistently meeting their customers' expectations. That's not their job. Their job is to help create and communicate what your customers can expect.

As a B2B marketer, it's *your* job to ensure that your branding builds confidence – to ensure the expectations you set are matched by experiences.

As B2B companies become more and more visible to their markets, it's obvious that the brand *is* the company.

Brand unity: meeting expectations

Brand unity does not mean managing everything to do with your content marketing or ensuring that your corporate identity is correctly applied. Brand unity means making sure that you deliver on your promises. It is critical that you meet expectations.

You want unity so that you don't dilute the credibility of your brand messages and allow your overall market to form inconsistent and inaccurate perceptions of your company.

Problems with brand unity are caused when brand messages are at odds with the market's actual experiences of dealing with you – when experience doesn't match expectation.

Take the example of any one of the many companies out there that highlight their dedicated commitment to serving customers, but then fail miserably at meeting that expectation in *simple* tasks such as answering the phone and responding to enquiries. 'Our customers are kings' doesn't ring true when you're sent to voicemail jail, get cut off, call again, leave a message and still nobody gets back to you.

If you can't get the simple things right, what confidence can anybody have that you will be able to handle something a bit more complicated?

Managing market reflections within B2B environments is perhaps the most challenging – and frustrating – of all marketing's functions.

It can also be the most rewarding in terms of exerting a consistently positive impact on sales, margins and market share.

Which is, of course, what B2B marketing is all about. No matter what B2B business you are in, your brand is your real business.

The importance of 'being the brand' – and how to achieve this – is something we'll look at in detail in Chapter 8 (Marketing united).

But before we leave brands and branding for a while to look at other things, here's an interesting way to look at what you're doing with yours and what, perhaps, you *should* be doing.

NO MATTER WHAT B2B BUSINESS YOU ARE IN, YOUR BRAND IS YOUR REAL BUSINESS

CREATING YOUR BRAND: 'IDEALIZED REDESIGN'

In his book *Ackoff's Fables*, management consultant Russell Ackoff describes a problem-solving process he calls 'idealized redesign'.

Although not specifically related to branding, the process is relevant if you want to 'be the brand'. In the context of branding, here's a paraphrase of Ackoff's process:

Imagine that your brand and branding were destroyed last night, but everything else in the world remains the same. Now redesign your brand and how it comes to life – your branding – so as to eliminate the problems that face it. This redesign is subject to only two constraints: first, it must be practical and achievable, and secondly, it must obey the same constraints (such as budgets and resources) that currently apply.

In addition, it should be redesigned so that it can:
- improve itself by learning from its own experience
- adapt to a changing environment
- be improved through redesign in the future.

You can start this revealing process by describing the market reflections that are essential to consistently motivate buying that generates sales, builds market share and protects margins.

But next we're going to look at how to get customers to ask, as soon as possible, the Ultimate Question: 'Where do I sign?' This is the topic of Chapter 7 (Extra special delivery).

DIRECTIONS TO RESULTS

This chapter is so important because it will reveal your markets' opinions of your products, services and processes. Based on that knowledge, you can then begin the process of building positive perceptions that will generate sales-creating trust.

Directions to results for Chapter 6 will show you:
- *exactly what the market thinks your brand represents; this is for real, because this is your brand*
- *what needs to be done to ensure your brand and your branding generate complete confidence in buying from you.*

Follow these steps to get into the fast lane:
- What are the market reflections for your brand? To answer this question, make a list of what *you* think your brand represents to each of the audiences in your spheres of influence – and why they might think so.
- Now run a cross-check on this question with the audiences: What do *they* see when they look at your brand – and what are the reasons for their perceptions? This is seriously important because the reflections tell you exactly what your company represents in the market. Just like Big John Rancher said in this chapter, this is what you own. Right now, this *is* your brand.
- What do all the people who deal with customers think your brand represents? Do opinions vary? Make a list and then ask yourself whose opinions need to change in order to present a *united* brand to the market. (We saw how important this unity is on page 101.)
- Now that you have a picture of what the market thinks of you – and what your company thinks of itself – you need to answer two critical questions:

1. What must your brand represent in order to build the confidence that will motivate buying from you?
2. What are the expectations that you must meet for customers in terms of your branding? List all the ways in which your brand comes to life through the experiences it creates for customers.

The process of 'idealized redesign' on page 102 will help you answer both questions.

Keep this list. It will be important when we get to Chapter 8 (Marketing united) and look at your performance in terms of keeping your brand promises right across your business.

7

Extra special delivery: right channels, right message, right people

A FAST TRACK TO THE ULTIMATE QUESTION –
'WHERE DO I SIGN?'

Coming up in this chapter:
- The Ultimate Question: 'Where do I sign?'
  - Faster money: accelerating B2B buying cycles
  - It's a very 'persona' matter: Who's who in the buying cycle?
  - Typical questions that lead up to the Ultimate Question
- Are your answers loud and clear?
  - Content, formats and channels
  - Search ... and rescue: why SEO will rescue your content from oblivion
  - First impressions: make sure yours are good

THE ULTIMATE QUESTION: 'WHERE DO I SIGN?'

'Where do I sign?' – it's the question every B2B company wants to hear. They want to hear it as often as possible and they want to be hearing it a lot more than their competitors.

It's your job as a B2B marketer to encourage, assist and motivate customers to move through the buying cycle towards the moment where they ask: 'Where do I sign?'

The Ultimate Question might be the last in a long list of questions from B2B buyers that need answering. It might be the easiest question to answer, but it's *the* question you want customers to ask.

Faster money: accelerating B2B buying cycles

If all the buyer's preceding questions in the cycle have been answered – as promptly as possible – in a way that is credible and relevant to all involved, then the Ultimate Question will be asked sooner rather than later.

This means you will have accelerated the buying cycle, cut your cost-of-sale by saving time and increased the customer's confidence in you.

From Chapter 5 (Content is king!) you know how to create marcoms content that motivates buying because it's credible and relevant to each of the audiences in your overall B2B market. And you have translated your content into the language of the Big Five buying motivators: response, service, time, quality and price.

You now need to make sure that your content is visible in the overall market and that it answers the questions that build confidence in buying from you.

To do so, you need to work through the various stages of the buying cycle to ensure that everyone with a question is receiving credible, relevant answers. Answers that are loud and clear.

B2B buying doesn't happen on a sudden impulse. It's a cycle that typically includes the six phases that we looked at in Chapter 5. See the diagram on the next page for a quick recap.

There will be different people, with different interests and responsibilities, involved in the cycle throughout its different phases. In Chapter 1

			B2B buying cycle		
Start					Finish
Phase 1	**Phase 2**	**Phase 3**	**Phase 4**	**Phase 5**	**Phase 6**
Identifying needs	Setting criteria	Specific research	Evaluation and testing	Selecting suppliers and negotiating	Buying and implementing

(The big, big market) you populated your sphere of influence and worked out who influences buying decisions.

In the same chapter you also considered that B2B buying is both strictly business and very personal.

To accelerate the buying cycle and get buyers to ask the Ultimate Question as soon as possible, you need to answer the right questions at the right time for the right people, which means we need to get personal ...

It's a very 'persona' matter: Who's who in the buying cycle?

The more you know about the people involved in each of the six phases, the easier it is to address their concerns. Talk about their favourite wines, their kids' school, their golf handicap and their plans for the holidays is all very salesy and friendly. But as a B2B marketer with the task of creating sales, protecting margins and building market share, you need to provide customers with information that will build confidence in buying. From you.

You need to create a profile – or to use a bit of buzzy marketing jargon, a 'persona' – that includes details of who they are, what they do, their degree of influence on buying decisions and what they need from you to create a positive attitude towards your products and services.

This is critically important because they are the people in the buying cycle who create your sales, protect your margins and build your market share.

Some of the information for a persona is straightforward: name, age, company, industry sector, business unit, responsibilities, reporting structures up and down, and likes and dislikes.

But you also need to add critical information about buying:

- How do they find out what they need to know during the buying cycle?
- What are their preferred information sources and formats?
- What gets their attention and makes them want to learn more?
- What are their tasks throughout the buying cycle and what results must they produce?
- What is their level of knowledge about what they're buying?
- How accurate is their knowledge and perception of your products and services?
- What are they specifically looking for based on their responsibilities?
- Where do they fit in the buying cycle?
- How much influence do they have on the Ultimate Question: 'Where do I sign?'
- *Most importantly, you need to figure out how all this information relates to the Big Five buying motivators. What are their expectations for response, service, time, quality and price? You need to find out!*

Fortunately, it is really easy to answer the last question: you can pull critical information about what motivates their buying straight from the results of the value analysis process that you sorted in Chapter 4 (Working with buying motivators).

How you build these personas is up to you. Your sales team may already have contact sheets that record who they're dealing with and what's going on. These might be a good starting point.

Capturing all persona information and keeping it up to date is the easy part. It's simply a matter of good record keeping on what's happening in your market and what's happening within and around customers.

What's more difficult is to apply all the information so that customers ask the Ultimate Question as soon as possible.

To simplify this task, let's look at the types of questions that need answering during the B2B buying cycle.

Typical questions that lead up to the Ultimate Question

When – and if – the Ultimate Question is asked depends on the credibility and relevance of all the answers that lead up to it. Here are the typical questions to which B2B buyers need answers.

Phase 1 Identifying needs	**Insight-Based Content**
	What are the trends, developments and challenges in my industry and my line of business? How are companies like us responding to them? Who really understands how this might contribute to our success? What related problems and consequences do we need to resolve and foresee? Are we risking our ability to compete by not doing this? What could I achieve for the company and myself by learning more about all of this?

Phase 2 Setting criteria	**Knowledge-Based Content**
	What support and resources would we need to buy and implement? How can we justify allocating the support and resources? If we go down this route, who else needs to be involved internally and externally? Are companies like us getting the results they expected? How would those results help us and what's the ROI? What would we need from a supplier to achieve those results / ROI?

Phase 3 Specific research	**Fact-Based Content**
	How are the various suppliers rated by people and info sources I know and trust? How do their products, services and processes actually work? What results are they delivering to companies like us? Who are those companies buying from? What are the likely total costs to us – in terms of time, resources, money? Who understands how to get results for users like us?

Phase 4 Evaluation and testing	**Evidence-Based Content**
	How can I test the products in an environment like ours? Who can organise this? Who can I talk to about their experiences of using the services I need? How can the final, total costs be clearly justified and approved? What are all the consequences of using these products and services? What are the must-have results we need and what's not essential? How will suppliers prove their ability to work with us to get the must-have results?

Phase 5 Selecting suppliers and negotiating	**Reinforcing Content**
	What's the ROI time frame? Why should I buy right now? Do the suppliers' terms & conditions conform to our rules? How financially stable are the suppliers? Do they have the necessary resources to meet the expectations they've created? What are the lead times on getting everything up and running?

Phase 6 Buying and implementing	**Fulfilment Content**
	There aren't any surprises in this contract, are there? There isn't any tricky stuff in the small print, is there? You are perfectly clear, aren't you, about exactly what you're contracting to do for me? You understand the non-performance clauses, don't you?

WHEN – AND IF – THE ULTIMATE QUESTION GETS ASKED DEPENDS ON THE CREDIBILITY AND RELEVANCE OF ALL THE ANSWERS THAT LEAD UP TO IT

ARE YOUR ANSWERS LOUD AND CLEAR?

You already have some great ideas for content from Chapter 5 (Content is king!). It's relevant and it's credible. The question now is how to get your content seen, consumed and appreciated by the people who make and influence buying decisions.

Strong answers to the questions buyers ask during the B2B buying cycle are all very well and good. But the answers don't matter unless they're *visible*.

Visibility means you need to look at marcoms channels – the routes you take to get the right answers to the right people. Here's a list of the typical marcoms channels in B2B.

Typical marcoms channels in B2B

- Industry, association and professional media
- General newspapers and magazines
- Search engines and search engine optimisation (SEO)
- Websites, and all the digital that goes with them
- Direct: email and newsletters
- Brochures and 'paperwork'
- Radio
- TV (Adverts? Maybe not. PR? Maybe yes.)
- Resellers, distributors, partners
- One-to-one: *anyone* who talks to customers
- Live events
- Social media
- User groups and forums
- Industry and sector peers: word-of-mouth (WOM)
- *Special mention: peer-to-peer*

The *peer-to-peer* channel gets a special mention because it has an important influence on B2B buying decisions. In fact, it can be the single most important influence of all. For example, if you want to buy a new laptop, who would you trust most to steer you in the right direction: in-store salespeople or everyone you know who raves about what they use?

Word-of-mouth, or WOM, is clearly an important channel. At first glance, it might not appear to be as structured and formal as the other channels because nobody actually sells it as a commodity, like print adverts or pay-per-click ads – but that doesn't mean you can't *manage* it.

Happy customers, user groups, online forums, social media and live events all provide an opportunity to turn WOM into a managed channel that encourages positive peer-to-peer interactions.

Because WOM has a significant influence on motivating buying decisions, we'll take a detailed look at it in Chapter 9 (PR and B2B: the perfect couple).

But let's first look at how to use B2B's marcoms channels to create that all-important visibility by matching the format of your content to the channels that deliver it. It's not difficult to do.

Content, formats and channels

It's pretty much common sense that you should present your content in a format that suits the delivery channels your audience prefers. Think about the diagram below:

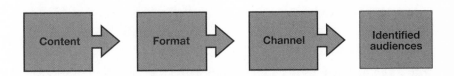

Let's say your CEO has been video-interviewed by a respected and widely read trade journal. It's a great piece of content that demonstrates a clear understanding of the challenges facing your sector and how your organisation is addressing them.

How are you (with the journal's permission) going to make this piece of content even more visible? Well, in its current video format you could load it onto your website and YouTube it.

But you could also change the format to suit more channels and reach more audiences. You could turn it into a mini white paper by producing a well-designed PDF transcript with some striking graphics that highlight the key points.

This could then form the basis for PowerPoint presentations for your sales team and at live events. You could feature it on your blog, include a bullet-point summary in a newsletter, create a mini email campaign and newscast it across social media and user groups.

Which means you need to be thinking simultaneously about content, formats, channels and audiences. And to help you do that, here's another list, of typical content and formats.

Content

- White papers, media articles
- Tests, research, surveys and analyst reports
- Case studies and best-practice guides
- Company profile
- Product and service data
- Pricing guides, ROI and cost-of-ownership

Formats

- Presentations and live events
- Web tools and apps
- Videos, webinars, podcasts, blogs
- Brochures, ebooks, emails, manuals, data sheets
- Social media snippets and 'factoids'
- Infographics and illustrations
- *Special mention: search and SEO*

Search and SEO get a special mention because they are often overlooked as a type of digital format in their own right. If you want to be visible digitally, then your content needs to be packaged in a way that makes it easy to find.

Search … and rescue: why SEO will rescue your content from oblivion

Back in Chapter 2 (Things *are* what they used to be), we looked at how the information superhighway enables self-educated buying decision makers to sell to themselves. From Google searches through to online user groups, B2B buyers build impressions and draw conclusions about your company long before they even consider making contact with you.

This self-selling behaviour undermines the effectiveness of all your sales team's efforts. Because they no longer need contact with your salespeople, customers are making decisions on their own.

For buyers, the attraction of independently sourcing digital information lies in its always-on convenience and its range of communication options, which span words, images, sounds, actions and interactions.

If your content is not digitally visible, you run the risk of being out of sight and out of mind. And out of the game!

But the rise of digital channels doesn't mean the fall of traditional ones.

Traditional channels, such as trade publications, live events, newspapers, magazines and radio, are still very much in the mix. The point to remember is that you need to be visible wherever the overall market is looking.

So the question today isn't whether to go digital or traditional. It's which channels you should choose that are most appealing to, trusted by and familiar to the people who are influencing decisions in the B2B buying cycle.

Then, the format of your content has to fit the channels you choose, because digital simply *is* different to traditional.

Clever software that converts Word documents – your white papers and case studies, for example – into PDFs does *not* mean you are now sorted digitally. Even clever software can't turn traditional into digital.

That's why we're taking a detailed look at all things digital in Chapter 10 (Digital, digital, digital: practical tactics to turn pixels into profits).

THE RISE OF DIGITAL DOESN'T MEAN TRADITIONAL CHANNELS ARE OBSOLETE

First impressions: make sure yours are good

In the first three phases of the buying cycle, buyers are gathering information to build knowledge about products, services and suppliers that might reinforce the success of their organisation.

They may simply be keeping themselves aware of what's happening in their field – engaging in a sort of professional window-shopping – or they may be responding to a more immediate need and taking the first steps towards buying a solution.

Either way, you need to be digitally visible. If you're not visible, you won't be seen as relevant and you won't be seen as credible. In fact, you simply won't be seen.

If buyers contact you in phase 4 – evaluation and testing – then it's fair to say that your content has been visible and it has been relevant. Why else would anyone want to trial your product or validate your services if they're irrelevant to their organisation?

At this point in the cycle – phase 4 – a buyer's focus shifts to looking for evidence that proves the capabilities of your products and services. So the focus of your content needs to shift to being factually credible.

It's also at this point that your organisation will probably start dealing with a larger group of people involved in the decision-making process. Some of these people may only have had a high-level briefing or summary of why the evaluation is happening. They are the late entrants into the buying cycle. Often they hold high levels of purchasing authority.

While your content has to emphasise your credibility, it also needs to be relevant to the late-entrant decision makers' interests and build confidence in buying from you. Of course, you already know who these people are likely to be, because you figured that out back in Chapter 1, when you populated your spheres of influence.

LATE ENTRANTS INTO THE BUYING CYCLE OFTEN HOLD HIGH LEVELS OF PURCHASING AUTHORITY

Late-entrant decision makers might be guided by the opinions of others, but they will still draw their own conclusions and make their own judgements. As senior decision makers or purchasing professionals, that's what they do. So creating positive first impressions that build confidence is clearly important.

From this point onwards in the cycle, your content needs to be readily available. It needs to be ready right now for handing out in meetings or for digital distribution. It needs to be visible for people who are preparing to select suppliers, negotiate and ask the Ultimate Question: 'Where do I sign?'

Because the last three phases of the buying cycle are typically handled by your sales team, this is a good time to look at how marketing must work together with everyone who comes into contact with customers.

That's what is coming up next, in Chapter 8 (Marketing united).

DIRECTIONS TO RESULTS

You are now seriously starting to build up speed in the fast lane to results. It might look like there's a lot to do here, but there isn't – you're merely pulling things together from the previous chapters. This is great, because you're capitalising on work that's already been done. And you're accelerating towards creating profitable sales.

Directions to results for Chapter 7 will show you:
- *how to build a rock-solid knowledge bank on what motivates your influencers to buy*
- *how to get the right messages to the right people all the way through the B2B buying cycle – from when they show initial interest to when they sign on the dotted line.*

Follow these steps to get into the fast lane:
- Choose a customer and create a persona that includes the straightforward contact and business details for *each* person who influences buying decisions. (You already have most of this information from Chapter 1, when you populated your spheres of influence.) Be sure to include influencers outside the customer, such as media commentators and consultants.
- For each influencer, add details that relate specifically to buying. You can check these on page 107. Then list their expectations in terms of the Big Five buying motivators.
- Now start to list how you will answer each influencer's questions in the buying cycle. You can use the list of typical questions on page 109 to guide you here.
- Add a list of the channels and the reasons you think these will reach each of the influencers.

- The final thing you need to do for each persona is to run a quick content check. Do you have all the content that each influencer needs to build their confidence in buying from you? Is all the content ready to go and is it currently relevant?
- Then repeat the exercise for other customers.

Creating a knowledge bank of buying-related personas is certainly not hard – but it takes time. So make this a positive habit rather than a negative chore. The process of creating personas will become easier and faster as you get used to selecting the important information and dumping anything that has no relevance to buying decisions.

8

Marketing united: singing the same song

Coming up in this chapter:
- Is everyone pulling in the same direction?
  - The customer's experience is king
  - Keep them coming back for more
- Move towards marketing united
  - How marketing makes money: four elevator pitches
  - We're all marketers now. So who's in charge?
  - Be careful what you promise

IS EVERYONE PULLING IN THE SAME DIRECTION?

The divide between marketing and sales has been talked to death. And if you think that this divide is a big divide, have a look at the ones that typically separate marketing from production, support, finance, distribution and IT.

Is everyone pulling in the same direction? Er, probably not!

This is a short chapter. It refers to many of the B2B marketing principles and practices covered so far. And it's short because it only needs to make one point: your entire business is about serving marketing's purpose.

Much of the traditional friction between marketing and other areas of business stems from the fact that marketers can be poor communicators when it comes to explaining marketing's purpose. But here's an explanation that everyone can understand: the purpose of marketing is to attract and retain profitable customers.

Anyone from anywhere in your company who contributes to that purpose is consequently part of the marketing function.

This concept of marketing as a function that spans right across the business is hardly new. Back in 1954, the doyen of management consultants Peter Drucker saw marketing like this: 'It encompasses the entire business. It is the whole business seen from the point of view of its final result, that is from the customer's point of view. Concern and responsibility for marketing must therefore permeate all areas of the enterprise.'

The entire business should be focused on ensuring that the customer's point of view is as positive as possible.

In Chapter 6 (Brands and branding), we looked at this simple fact: *Brands create expectations, branding creates experiences.*

Your *brand* represents what you do, how you do it and why you matter to customers. Your branding represents all of this in action: it concerns the way in which you turn your brand into customer experience.

How customers see your company is a combination of their expectations and their experiences. To create a positive customer view, your entire business has to ensure that what the customer expects is what the customer gets. Because this is what creates sales, protects margins and increases market share.

This means that everyone who affects the customer experience has to work together in a united effort to *be* the brand. This raises an old and thorny truism: anyone who doesn't have a positive effect on the customer experience doesn't have a positive effect on your company's success. So why are they still there if their only contribution is to increase your overheads?

THE PURPOSE OF MARKETING IS TO ATTRACT AND RETAIN PROFITABLE CUSTOMERS

The customer's experience is king

If you want to *be* the brand, you have to introduce customers to the people who will contribute to their experience. Everyone who has an effect on customers should be getting to know them – as people.

Why should you do this? Because customers are not an inanimate line on a sales graph, or a percentage of revenue, or a level of profit ability, or a production target. They're people.

Your engineers need to be meeting their engineers, your finance people need to be talking to their finance people, and your production managers need to be rolling up their sleeves alongside their counterparts.

Where do we meet your expectations? And where do we let you down?

It's a lot harder for people to duck their customer-experience responsibilities if they've met customers face to face, have had some coffee or a drink together and found they have something in common. Such customer interaction needs to be formally managed in a structured, scheduled process that has a single purpose: to build sales and protect margins by consistently striving to deliver a positive customer experience – an experience that keeps encouraging customers to come back for more.

Keep them coming back for more

In Chapter 3 (B2B's Big Five buying motivators), we looked at what really makes customers buy. Let's do a quick recap of two of these motivators to see how they relate to this broad-based interaction with customers.

Response

Response stands right at the top of the list of buying motivators. The continual dialogue with customers reveals how you can help build their success by understanding their challenges and by collaborating to solve them.

This dialogue has to extend beyond a sales team that's driven by getting another order. It has to involve all the people – in engineering, production, logistics, R&D, finance and support – who contribute to meeting expectations and enhancing the customer experience.

Customers need to see this as a genuine commitment towards building their success – not some slickly phrased lip service to being customer-centric or customer-focused.

Service

Service is number two on the list of buying motivators. Customers need reassurance that you are proactively sharing your knowledge about best practices, industry trends, developments, emerging challenges and the experiences of your other, similar, customers. Your service must demonstrate that you have the customer's best interests at heart.

Once again, everyone who is delivering the customer experience needs to be making their contribution towards strengthening a long-term, win-win relationship with customers by understanding their expectations and fulfilling them.

MOVE TOWARDS MARKETING UNITED

The point about collaborating internally brings us back to the concept of 'marketing united'. There's no point in building knowledge about customers' expectations unless they are matched by experiences.

If you want your marketing to build sales and protect margins, it is essential that marketers talk to colleagues in other departments about the company's common purpose and the contributions everyone needs to make to enhance customers' experiences.

Almost twenty years after explaining that marketing needs to be regarded as the top priority right across the company, Peter Drucker reinforced his long-held opinion on its purpose like this: 'The aim of marketing is to know and understand the customer so well that the product or service fits him and sells itself. Ideally, marketing should result in a customer who is ready to buy.'

And who doesn't want that?!

So get united and convince everyone in authority that marketing really is all about making profitable sales. Let's look at what you might want to say to convince them.

How marketing makes money: four elevator pitches

Pitch number 1: consistent sales

Selling becomes hard if you don't understand the products and services that customers want.

Understanding your customers – or 'customer insight' – is clearly a vital component in selling products and services that the market wants to buy.

Without marketing's insight into customers, your company is building a formidable barrier to generating profitable sales.

SELLING IS HARD IF YOU DON'T UNDERSTAND THE PRODUCTS AND SERVICES THAT CUSTOMERS VALUE

Pitch number 2: higher profits

You can't protect margins if you don't understand all the reasons why customers want a product or service.

A lack of customer insight blinds you when setting margins based on the value your products and services deliver. In terms of price management and value pricing, it is essential that your company understands how you support your customers' success.

Without this understanding, you're left with nothing more than a 'cost-plus' approach to pricing. Your margins – and therefore your profits – will remain under pressure because you're not leveraging the value you create. Instead, you're selling on price.

YOU CAN ONLY PROTECT MARGINS IF YOU UNDERSTAND WHY CUSTOMERS WANT A PRODUCT OR SERVICE

Pitch number 3: beating competitors

You won't attract and keep customers if they can't see how you're different from all the rest.

Sidelining the competition, so that customers buy from you and not from anyone else, obviously has an impact on sales: they will increase! That's why it is important to *differentiate* yourself from the competition.

Relevant, credible and visible marcoms ensure that the whole market clearly understands why buying from you is the right choice.

YOU WILL ONLY ATTRACT AND KEEP CUSTOMERS IF THEY CAN SEE HOW YOU DIFFER FROM ALL THE REST

Pitch number 4: product development

Customers don't buy square pegs for round holes. So don't develop a world-class square peg if your customer needs round pegs.

B2B customers buy products and services that will make them more successful. Understanding what motivates their buying – what they value – has to be an important consideration in developing new products and services.

Development must also be guided by what customers will value in the future – in order to respond successfully to future trends and challenges.

DON'T DEVELOP A WORLD-CLASS SQUARE PEG IF YOUR CUSTOMERS NEED TO FILL ROUND HOLES

We're all marketers now. So who's in charge?

If everyone in the company plays a part in marketing by making positive contributions to the customer experience, then the responsibility for marketing lies with everyone.

This is a neat thought. It means that the entire organisation is focused on creating a consistently positive experience for delighted customers ('Summertime ... sales are jumpin' and the margins are high ...').

The problem is that when everybody is responsible, nobody is accountable. That's when things could go pear-shaped.

Thankfully, this is a problem with a logical and practical solution. The solution is based on creating value for customers across the Big Five buying motivators: response, service, time, quality and price.

Here are two examples of how to link accountability to value:

- Is the problem due to little understanding of customer needs and a failure to address them? As a result, are revenues static or falling? This sounds like a *response* problem created by marketing and sales – so they must fix it by talking to customers and finding out what they really need.
- Are customers consistently complaining about erratic lead times and threatening to look elsewhere? Clearly, this is a *time* issue. It could be a production problem, so the production department must sort it out directly with the customer. If production is the cause of the problem, they must face the music – not some poor Johnny-in-the-middle from after-sales support.

Be careful what you promise

Empty promises that your business cannot keep are a sure-fire way to disappoint and lose customers. If you create great expectations, then you have to back them up with great experiences.

So marcoms should tell the whole truth about how you create value for customers by understanding and meeting their expectations. We dealt with creating value in Chapter 4 (Working with buying motivators).

We also dealt with the issue of telling the whole truth in Chapter 5 (Content is king!). We looked at how your content must describe every single way in which you contribute to your customers' success, in such a way that it's relevant and credible to each person's position and function within the buying cycle. We also explored how to translate all your marcoms into language that motivates buying.

The danger with B2B marcoms is that marketers often diverge from the rigorous discipline of telling the whole truth. Usually they do this because they don't know it – and that is why they lapse into the hyperbole and fantasy-infested world of B2C marcoms. In the cautionary words of singer-songwriter Bob Dylan, this is the world that tries to 'con you into thinking you're the one that can do what's never been done, that can win what's never been won'.

It is bad enough if the rest of your business doesn't think your marketing content is relevant or credible and therefore refuses to take you seriously. It's even worse if the market thinks the same.

So be careful what you promise the market.

One of the ways in which you can make promises is through PR. This is the focus of Chapter 9 (PR and B2B: the perfect couple).

DIRECTIONS TO RESULTS

You need to be careful when positioning marketing's role within the company. It's certainly not a good idea to tell your colleagues that marketing is more important than what they do. It's much better to explain that marketing is an important part of what they do.

Directions to results for Chapter 8 will show you:
- *everyone who affects the customer experience within your company and whether they're having a positive effect on sales*
- *who is responsible for creating customer experiences that consistently attract and retain profitable customers*
- *how to discover where you're meeting customer expectations and where you're not*
- *how to entrench marketing as the top responsibility for anyone who interacts with customers.*

Follow these steps to get into the fast lane:
- Make a list of everyone who deals with customers (and I mean *everyone*: from the front desk to the boardroom). This is your customer interaction list.
- Create four elevator pitches to explain marketing's purpose to everyone on your customer interaction list. Use the examples on pages 123–5 to guide your four pitches, but write them for *your* company and *your* colleagues.
- Write down who is responsible for what in terms of delivering on the Big Five (response, service, time, quality and price). Use the examples on page 126 to guide you. Keep this list, as you will come back to it in Chapter 11, when you will look at measuring marketing's direct contribution to creating profitable sales.

- Now run a reality check on customer expectations vs. customer experiences: Where are you getting it right and where is it going wrong? Keep this list too, as you'll also be coming back to it in Chapter 11.

9

PR and B2B: the perfect couple

MANAGING COMMUNICATIONS THAT GENERATE SALES-CREATING TRUST

Coming up in this chapter:
- Countering the challenges of 'orchestrated lying'
  - PR in B2B: What is it and what is its role?
  - PR: building trust that leads to sales
  - Market exposure: paid, earned and owned
  - Creating trust across all your audiences
- Layers of influence, layers of communication
- Using a PR agency: yes or no?
  - Briefing for results
  - Leverage your skills, leverage agency skills
- Are they talking about us? Harnessing word-of-mouth (WOM)
  - Cultivating WOM through live events
  - If you build it, surely they will come?
  - Using events to boost direct contact with your markets

COUNTERING THE CHALLENGES OF 'ORCHESTRATED LYING'

With all the many deceitful messages pumped at us by B2C brands, it's hardly surprising that it's really tough for B2B companies to generate sales-creating trust in their messages.

B2C advertising might be high-profile, high-frequency, high-reach and fabulously packaged, but because much of it falls into the category of 'orchestrated lying', we don't trust much of it. We may even have reached the point where we don't trust *any* of it.

Corporate trend analyst Dion Chang had this to say about trust in the final South African edition of the B2C marketing magazine *AdVantage*, in 2013: 'For modern day consumers, their trust in corporate companies, brands and advertising messages has been eroded to such an extent that it has become a rare commodity, altering completely the brand building mission.'

Thanks to all the ridiculous nonsense that we are fed by B2C brands, we're rightfully wary of brand-building propaganda. We recognise that these everyday deceits are only adverts. And we don't trust them, do we? Of course not. Nobody *trusts* them. They certainly aren't trusted by the people who hold the responsibility associated with major business buying decisions – the very people you're targeting with your marketing activities.

A consequence of the widespread scepticism created by B2C baloney is that all forms of product promotion get tarred with the same brush. One way to counter this scepticism is to steer clear of anything that smacks of a B2C con story.

If the messages in your content look or sound anything like an advert for something you'd buy in a supermarket, then maybe it is time to change them.

Not all B2C advertising falls into the con category. Honest products can be and are marketed in honest ways. Niall FitzGerald, a past chairman of the consumer goods giant Unilever, said in 2001: 'Among the first to appreciate William Lever's Sunlight soap were those who had so little money that there was no such thing as a trivial purchase.

Any mistake was a serious mistake. Sunlight saved them from painful error.' Avoidance of painful error is truly a high priority in the B2B buying process.

Everyone involved needs to be certain that buying from you is the right decision. They need to trust you.

We covered the process of building trust in your brand in Chapter 6 (Brands and branding). PR plays a leading role in that trust-building process.

AVOIDANCE OF PAINFUL ERROR IS A HIGH PRIORITY IN THE B2B BUYING PROCESS

PR in B2B: what is it and what is its role?

The role of PR in B2B is to provide relevant and credible answers to the question, 'Why should customers be 100 per cent confident that buying from you is the right decision?'

Before we look at what PR involves, we need to acknowledge that the term itself – public relations – lacks a precise definition. Some see it as dealing primarily with the media, that is, with press relations and publicity. Others regard it as handling what is known as 'corporate communications', both with the outside world and within the company. In 2012, the Public Relations Society of America provided this definition: 'Public relations is a strategic communication process that builds mutually beneficial relationships between organizations and their publics.'

In the United Kingdom, the Chartered Institute of Public Relations sees it in slightly plainer terms: 'Public Relations is about reputation – the result of what you do, what you say and what others say about you. Public Relations is the discipline which looks after reputation, with the aim of earning understanding and support and influencing opinion and behaviour. It is the planned and sustained effort to establish and maintain goodwill and mutual understanding between an organisation and its publics.'

Both definitions talk about PR being a structured, continuing process of communication. Both imply that this is a good thing, because it creates positive perceptions about the organisation. And both say these perceptions are created among an organisation's 'publics'.

The term 'publics' is jargon for the various elements that comprise the community in which an organisation operates. In reality, it includes everyone the organisation addresses.

In marketing-speak, this translates to the community of audiences that form your overall market – the influencers within your spheres. Take your community very seriously: it's your only source of sales. The role of PR is to build sales-creating trust within it.

THE ROLE OF PR IS TO BUILD SALES-CREATING TRUST WITHIN YOUR COMMUNITY

PR: building trust that leads to sales

While 'orchestrated lying' leaves B2B buying decision makers cold, they're certainly hot on hearing other people's experiences and recommendations – that is, if they trust them.

They will start taking an interest in you when a media source they respect runs a story on successes that similar companies are achieving with your products or services. They will visit websites that appear relevant and credible at the top of a Google search. Provided they trust you to contribute to their success, customers and prospects will attend your events, download your white papers and respond to your advertising. If they think you're merely producing propaganda, they won't.

In B2B, buying decision makers are looking for exposure to content that is informative, credible and relevant to where they are in the buying cycle. And it is PR's job to make sure you get that exposure.

Market exposure: paid, earned and owned

There are three types of exposure that PR – as opposed to advertising – can generate for your brand: you can pay for PR exposure, you can earn it, or you can own it.

Which of these you choose should depend on the measurable outcome it will produce – in terms of profitable sales.

Paid PR exposure might be a live event you organise or sponsor. It could also be a special-offer campaign or a competition.

Earned PR exposure includes editorial coverage, word-of-mouth (including social media), endorsements, recommendations and invitations to speak at seminars and conferences or to submit content to an industry association or to a blog.

Some people talk about 'shared' exposure as a distinct category, but to be shared it first needs to have earned the right to be shared.

Search engine optimisation (SEO) is also earned in the sense that search engines recognise your content's relevance to particular search terms.

Owned PR exposure relates to all the content that appears on your own channels. This includes your website, your direct-contact campaigns and your hard-copy collateral (the range of marketing material used to increase awareness of a product or service). It also includes all people internally who contribute to a positive customer experience and reinforce trust across all your audiences.

Creating trust across all your audiences

B2B buying decisions are influenced by many different people, who together make up your overall market. In Chapter 1 (The big, big market), you looked at who those people might be within a sphere of influence. Let's do a quick recap on some key issues about people who influence buying decisions:

- Besides direct customers or end users, a typical B2B sphere is populated by commentators in the media, wholesalers and distributors, overall solution providers, specialist consultancies or professions, and support and service providers.
- It may also include other buying-decision influencers such as user groups, industry analysts, shareholders, trade associations and the general public.
- Each audience is a target for communications that build trust in your products and services.
- The fact that there are multiple audiences within overall B2B markets means you can't have catchy, one-size-fits-all brand messages. Your PR must deliver messages that are credible and relevant to *each* audience.

In Chapter 7 (Extra special delivery), we looked at how to use various channels to get the right messages to the right people at the right time in the B2B buying cycle. And we covered how to formulate the content of those messages in Chapter 5 (Content is king!). A key message in that chapter was this: *Building confidence through relevance and credibility is directly linked to building sales and protecting margins.*

The more confidence – that is, the more trust – you can instil in everyone who influences buying decisions, the more likely you are to sell your products and services. So, within the PR function, it's important to understand the varying degrees of influence exerted by different people at different phases of the buying cycle.

YOUR PR MUST DELIVER MESSAGES THAT ARE CREDIBLE AND RELEVANT TO EACH AUDIENCE

LAYERS OF INFLUENCE, LAYERS OF COMMUNICATION

Not all influencers are equal. That's why it makes sense to categorise them in layers of influence and assign a PR target to each one. You then need to decide what response you want from each of the layers and plan how to get it.

The plan will define the frequency of communication for each layer, the delivery channel and the type of content. People in the most influential layer need to be treated differently from those with less influence.

For example, perhaps your most senior managers or execs should share news, views and experiences at regular meetings with the top tier of influencers. As the influence decreases in the lower layers, so can the frequency and intensity of your communications.

The type of content will also vary according to its target layer – its audience. If you're in the stainless-steel supply game, your invitation list for a seminar about the factors affecting future demand for stainless steel will differ from that for a practical workshop on stainless-steel welding.

The PR goal, though, is the same: to build a community of positive influencers who are confident that you contribute more to their success than your competitors.

YOUR PR GOAL IS TO BUILD A COMMUNITY OF POSITIVE INFLUENCERS WHO BELIEVE YOU CONTRIBUTE MORE TO THEIR SUCCESS THAN YOUR COMPETITORS

USING A PR AGENCY: YES OR NO?

'Cultivating communications is a job no public relations agency can do for a company.' This is the blunt opinion of Regis McKenna in his book *Relationship Marketing*. Published in 1991, it's about how to 'own the market through strategic customer relationships'. It is still seen as one of the most influential books on how to increase revenue and profits by being a customer-centric organisation.

Since he's a marketing consultant with a client list that reads like the who's who in Silicon Valley, it's worth listening to what McKenna has to say.

McKenna says that PR begins at home: it starts with senior managers and execs and how they handle their communications with all the audiences in the market, in a cohesive, same-song manner. This unified approach should be followed by everyone who deals with customers and prospective clients.

His opinion is that these communications cannot be managed by a third-party agency. It has to be handled person-to-person by people inside the company. Why? Because insiders know more than anyone about their products, services and processes. You saw in the previous chapter that everyone who affects the customer experience should be interacting with their counterparts within the customers' organisations. They should consider it a top priority to understand what customers value and what they don't.

The challenge when hiring an external agency to 'cultivate communications' is that it is difficult for outsiders to develop a true understanding of the three Ps – your purpose, your process and your promise – that we looked at in Chapter 2. These three Ps define:

- who you are
- what you do
- how you do it
- why you can do it and
- why all this really matters to customers.

Many PR agencies are woefully poor at uncovering these truths, which means they can't use them as a foundation to increase your sales and protect your margins.

Another inconvenient truth is that far too many agencies don't know enough about B2B marketing, let alone what motivates the business buying that creates profitable sales.

If an agency can't define how your content and channels relate to the buying cycle (or the buyers' journey, or the sales funnel, or whatever you want to call the B2B buying process), then you engage them at your peril.

It is important to consider what you might want a PR agency to do for you. Do you want them to write content? And if so, what type of content – press releases, white papers, insight pieces, technical manuals, brochures, web copy? Do you want them to be a route into the media? Or to select the channels that will reach your audiences?

You also need to answer this question: If you engage an agency, how will their work boost your revenue and profitability? In order to answer this question, it helps to set a very specific goal – profitable sales – and consider how an agency would apply its skills to achieve this goal.

This means you need to prioritise what you need to achieve, and write a clear brief that defines it.

Briefing for results

If ever there was a misnomer in PR it has to be the word 'brief': 'Sweetie, just nip round there and take the brief. Oh, and be an angel and pleeease pick up sushi on the way back.'

Understanding how to communicate with your audiences in a manner that creates sales is a big task. Developing such a crucial understanding doesn't merely require a once-off 'brief'; it needs a continual, interactive process between your company, the agency and your overall market.

The commercial problem here is that an agency is often being paid to learn all the reasons why the market should be 100 per cent confident in buying from you. And if *you* don't know all the reasons, then you will end up with a seriously dodgy case of the blind leading the blind.

The importance of the (not-so-brief) brief

'Turnover is vanity, profit is sanity, cash is reality' – this is not a bad mantra to keep in mind when defining how an agency will contribute to putting cash in your bank account. In fact, it should guide you in briefing an agency on what they need to achieve.

'Awareness' is often cited as one of the top results delivered by PR. Market awareness, brand awareness, product awareness.

The overall market may be *aware* of your products and services, but is it *buying* them? Awareness doesn't automatically turn into bankable cash. Simply creating awareness is not enough. It has to have a bankable goal. This once again means you have to be very clear about what you need your PR to achieve. You need to be specific about your goals.

A specific goal might be to increase profitable sales of a particular product or service within a particular market sector. This then needs to be linked to some targets: by what percentage must sales increase? At what margin? Over what period of time? Using what resources? And for what budget?

By setting such targets you will have created something that can be planned for in a PR campaign. In other words, you can define the activities that are necessary to achieve the targets. You can then put a price on those activities. It becomes a project that is managed within specific parameters to produce specific results.

Another issue is the importance of taking manageable steps and setting realistic goals. Don't try to do everything at once and don't try to do it overnight. It takes time to change entrenched opinions and preconceptions within your market. Trust and confidence are built one step at a time in a cumulative process of repeatedly being seen by your audiences as relevant and credible – as having a message that's worth listening to.

Leverage your skills, leverage agency skills

If you can change a light bulb yourself, why call an electrician? The same applies to using a PR agency. You need to decide which activities are yours and which are theirs. But never confuse activity with achievement.

Do not confuse activity with achievement

Writing a press release is not an achievement. Distributing the release is not an achievement. Having it published is not an achievement. Having it read by a new, budget-ready customer is not an achievement. Generating a lead from that customer is not an achievement. Responding to the lead, meeting the customer, running trials and submitting proposals are not achievements. These are all activities.

But: making a profitable, long-life sale to that customer is an achievement.

MAKING A PROFITABLE, LONG-LIFE SALE TO A CUSTOMER IS AN ACHIEVEMENT

And if sales don't happen, then what was the point of all that writing, distributing, publishing, lead generation and responding? More to the point, why wasn't the customer sufficiently confident to buy? What were the shortcomings in the activities that resulted in losing the sale? Was the message the problem, or how it was distributed, or who it targeted? Was the product the problem, or its availability, or its pricing? Was there something wrong with your response to the customer?

How you answer those questions is another matter. The answers to these questions deal with measurement, and we'll be looking at this critical function in Chapter 11 (Measuring the king).

But let's get back to our customer, who had a budget, asked for information, engaged with sales, ran a trial and read your proposal.

And then didn't buy.

In this scenario, the problem is that not everyone in the overall market was 100 per cent confident that buying from you was the right choice. And as long as your PR function allows that situation to persist, generating profitable sales as a direct result of PR activities is always going to be an uphill battle.

Here are some reasons. In Chapter 6 (Brands and branding), we saw how market reflections – the associations the market makes with your

141

brand – are what underpin a B2B company's ability to increase sales, protect margins and retain customers. The influence of market reflections is increasing rather than decreasing. For example, there is growing B2B interest in the significance of social media as a way for people to talk about their experiences of suppliers and products. This goes both ways: companies are joining in and encouraging the discussion in order to reinforce their brand messages and build market confidence.

In Chapter 8 (Marketing united), we looked at why it is so important for everyone who affects the customer experience to interact with customers – as people. This type of interaction needs to be extended to a top-down culture of talking to the overall market – not only customers or prospects but *all* the audiences that influence customers' buying decisions.

If an audience can influence buying decisions, your people need to be talking to them.

All this talk about talking brings us to one of the most influential B2B marcoms channels of all: word-of-mouth, or WOM.

ARE THEY TALKING ABOUT US?
HARNESSING WORD-OF-MOUTH (WOM)

Some years ago I wrote a blog post, 'The big WOM buzz', which looked at why social media was attracting such massive attention among marketers. The reason was simple: it was turning WOM into a monster comms channel.

In both B2C and B2B, WOM has always been hugely influential on buying decisions. From talking to friends and acquaintances about the best burger in town through to the next car we might buy, the influence of 'experienced others' – people we trust – carries immense weight in our buying decisions.

We rely on the opinions of people we trust and respect to build our own buying confidence. And this happens all the time. Who is talking and what they are saying has been made globally accessible by online communication channels. This matters to B2B marketers because these channels not only have enormous reach, they also have turned static information into active communication.

They have moved us from monologue to dialogue, from a one-way street to a two-way highway. This is digital WOM.

DIGITAL WOM HAS MOVED US FROM MONOLOGUE TO DIALOGUE, FROM A ONE-WAY STREET TO A TWO-WAY HIGHWAY

In Chapter 7 (Extra special delivery), we looked at the fact that nobody actually sells WOM as a commodity in the same way as print or pay-per-click adverts are sold.

WOM might not appear to be as structured a medium as other comms channels, but that doesn't mean you can't manage it. A good place to start managing WOM is to understand who is saying what about your industry, your company, your products and services, and your competitors.

Where they are saying it might span a wide range of channels: user groups, online forums, blogs, newsfeeds, industry portals, social media and throughout the press. All these channels provide an opportunity to turn WOM into a proactively managed medium that encourages positive peer-to-peer interactions.

WOM can only be managed successfully if all your insiders are actively delivering consistent, confidence-building messages to all your audiences. No PR agency can do the job of cultivating that consistency for your company.

Cultivating WOM through live events

Live events are certainly one of the most effective forms of marketing tactics. They offer an unparalleled opportunity to deliver relevant and credible messages directly to every audience in your spheres of influence.

They encourage your audiences to talk among themselves about why buying from you is such a smart move.

The significance of live events today is more important than ever before. This significance will continue to grow. Why? Because, as we saw in Chapter 5 (Content is king!), the one-to-one sales process – direct selling – is under severe pressure. Its influence is being diluted by internet-empowered customers who see no advantage in engaging with your sales team until late in the buying cycle. They're finding out what they need to know online and on their own.

As we saw when we explored the basic rules of B2B marketing in Chapter 2 (Things *are* what they used to be), direct selling has been pushed further and further towards the end of the cycle. Customers have pretty much decided where they're going and who's going with them – before having any direct contact with your sales staff.

Events provide a proactive means to counter the real and ever-present danger that is threatening the once-almighty B2B sales function. Events highlight your products and services during the initial phases of the buying cycle, when customers are still identifying needs, setting the criteria that govern how best to address those needs, and searching for products that will fulfil their needs.

Tried, tested, proven

Events have a long-standing reputation in B2B as a sure-fire way to generate leads that convert to profitable, long-life sales. Their ability to do so stretches back to the very first vendors who set out their wares in the very first marketplaces. So there's nothing newfangled or trendy or cutting-edge about events.

All the reasons why the market should buy from you can be distilled into a live event. They provide an at-a-glance opportunity for your market to see a perfectly formed, miniaturised version of your company. Audiences within your sphere of influence get a first-hand, face-to-face perspective of who you are, what you do, how you do it and why you should matter – to them.

If you are serious about generating profitable sales, you have to be serious about events.

Get some partners

Alliance marketing is a powerful way to show how your products and services fit into a multi-component product or service. At the same time, organising a range of events in partnership with your value-added resellers (VARs) or distributors spreads costs and demonstrates your commitment to building customers' success.

If you build it, surely they will come?

Er, no, they probably won't come. People who influence and make buying decisions won't attend events that don't benefit them. The main reason why they *will* attend your event is if they believe it will make a *measurable contribution* to their success and the success of their organisation. It has to be something they can act upon and that will help them achieve their goals.

Your goal must be to serve their goals

To achieve this goal, take a good look at the audiences in your spheres of influence. For each one, work out what you can present that will serve the decision makers' goals. Once you understand what it is, you can begin to think about the type of event that will serve *your* goals too – generating profitable sales.

Using events to boost direct contact with your markets

Here is a list of the type of events you might want to consider, together with some examples of their typical content and what they're good at achieving.

1. Seminars

Seminars are small events for relatively few senior managers. A typical example is a breakfast event for heavyweight influencers, at which you might explore the consequences of industry trends and developments, and how your products and services deal with these. They are best for presenting content that is focused on the first three phases of the buying cycle.

2. Product workshops

Workshops at which your products are showcased are good for attracting small numbers on a frequent, rotating basis – perhaps for twenty people every quarter. The focus is typically on people who are already working with your products as part of their job.

Workshops provide opportunities for hands-on demonstrations of tech features and performance, training in best operational practices and a variety of applications, and for reinforcing the operational reasons why your products are the right ones to buy.

Product workshops are also suitable for reinforcing customer retention and for upselling, as it will help you build your customers' confidence in the performance of all your products and services.

3. Round-table discussions

These events usually target senior managers from a specific industry or discipline, inviting them to share their opinions and experiences about particular challenges and how to best address them.

They are often organised and staged by trade media as a multi-company showcase of 'expert' opinions and insights on trends and developments.

Round-table discussions are particularly effective for positioning complex services through examples of real-world applications, and for demonstrating an in-depth understanding of market demands and how to meet them.

4. Party time

Parties provide a perfect opportunity to demonstrate your appreciation of customers' loyalty. Everybody likes to be thanked. From after-work drinks and snacks, through to golf days, sports events and corporate lunches, these events are all about saying thank you and strengthening the relationships that generate your revenue and profits.

They also provide a great opportunity to involve everyone who affects the customer experience, and to discover what's working for customers and what's not.

5. Roadshows

This means you take your company to the market. Roadshows can take the form of a seminar or a product workshop, or a party event; it might even cover all three at different times in the same location.

Roadshows are suitable for supporting VARs in different locations across the country, or for targeting clusters of same-industry customers and prospects. It is an effective means of introducing new products and upselling to your existing customer base.

6. Conferences

geted at existing customers (particularly distributors and agents) rather than at prospects. Conferences typically run for several days and attract several hundred delegates.

Conferences provide an opportunity to cover a wide range of topics across a broad range of market interests and offer a good platform for detailed case studies, analyses of best practices, explanations of product development plans, and as a heads-up on how best to respond to trends and developments.

7. Trade shows and exhibitions

Trade shows and exhibitions typically focus on a particular industry or profession, and usually take place annually. They often feature multiple companies, often direct competitors, in a dedicated exhibition environment.

These provide opportunities for the market to meet the people who drive your company beyond the day-to-day sales and support environment.

They are an ideal platform for clearly differentiating your company from the competition by showcasing real-world examples of how you build your customers' success.

Events are a way to counter the threats posed by the digital world, so it should be clear that you do need to understand how customers are using online resources during the buying cycle – and how to position yourself in that digital space. This will be coming up next, in Chapter 10, titled 'Digital, digital, digital: practical tactics to turn pixels into profits'.

DIRECTIONS TO RESULTS

PR is one of the most powerful ways to build your markets' trust in buying from you. This is why it is important to make sure that you use its power wisely.

Directions to results for Chapter 9 will show you:
- *how to use PR to build sales-creating trust in your markets*
- *how to define PR activities and link them to measurable results*
- *which PR activities are most likely to produce those results based on your resources (budgets, skills and time)*
- *how to initiate more direct, personal contact with the people who influence buying decisions.*

Follow these steps to get into the fast lane:
- Identify a specific result you want your PR to deliver. Simply saying that you want more sales is nowhere near specific enough. You need to think about precise targets, as described on page 139 (under the heading 'Briefing for results').
- Now define in detail the steps that will have to be taken – and who must take them – to be successful at achieving the result you want. For each step, what resources will you need in terms of time, money and skills?
- If you combine your listed targets and the steps to reach them, you will have a guiding template for planning your PR activities to achieve results.
- Consider ways in which you can use live events to increase direct contact with people within your spheres of influence. Go through all the different types of events covered on pages 145–8: Which ones are most likely to attract your target audience and move you closer to the results you need?

10

Digital, digital, digital

PRACTICAL TACTICS TO TURN PIXELS INTO PROFITS

Coming up in this chapter:
- The perfidious internet: digital is here to stay
  - The world's biggest companies are digital
- Three digital challenges
  - Visible, accessible and credible – or how to stand out
  - Metrics – using data to know your prospects and predict their behaviour
- Tactical marketing – pushing the pixel
  - Creating results through actions
  - Create your platforms and content
  - Reach your audience
  - Engage your prospects
  - Acquire business
  - Measure success
- What's coming down the pipe?
  - Immersive reality
  - Anonymity
  - The internet of things

THE PERFIDIOUS INTERNET: DIGITAL IS HERE TO STAY

It's everywhere, and you can't avoid it – the internet. So turn it to your advantage.

When was the last time you *didn't* use the internet? Probably when you were hiking in the Himalayas or diving in the Mariana Trench. Let's face it: it's almost impossible to find somewhere on the planet that doesn't have connectivity. And with the proliferation of smartphones and tablets, we're not only addicted to the web, but we're on it 24/7.

So are your customers. And they're using it to inform their buying decisions.

The world's biggest companies are digital

Late in 2014, Michael Brenner, the much-respected ex-VP of marketing at SAP, said that 'the B2B marketing organization of the future will be organized around data, content and technology'.

Brenner's observation is not surprising, given that the world's biggest companies are all connected in one form or another to tech, content and digital stuff. Take, for example, three of the most valuable businesses in history: Apple, Google and Microsoft. Many of the world's biggest companies are digital – and they're there to empower you.

On the surface, these organisations appear to be consumer brands. In reality, most of their revenues are derived from their B2B activities.

The truly amazing thing about them is that their sole purpose is to empower businesses such as yours to connect with your prospects. They open gateways to information and, through this, help shape the opinions of your buyers.

They're not doing it for charity either: they make money from this – heaps of money. So if they're not your friends already, you need to cosy on up to them, because they'll help you make money too.

THE WORLD'S BIGGEST COMPANIES ARE ALL CONNECTED TO TECH, CONTENT AND DIGITAL

In Chapter 2 (Things *are* what they used to be), we looked at McGraw-Hill's interpretation of the basic rules of B2B (the Man in the Chair advert) and saw that the fundamentals of being on-message haven't changed over the years. By contrast, the *way* in which the three most valuable digital companies (and others like them) have transformed how we create, deliver and access information has had some profound implications for the B2B marketer.

By way of example, Google runs over 40 000 search queries every second. That's 3.5 billion search queries a day. Its clever, spidery arms have crawled and indexed trillions of pages of content on the internet and they've done a pretty amazing job of ordering them into a usable filing cabinet – a Yellow Pages for the digitally connected.

If you have a website or you've posted some content to your social media platforms, chances are (unless your technical team messed up) that your content will be somewhere in that index.

The question is whether you'll be able to persuade Google to dig it up for the right people at the right time.

Through Bing, its business software suites, web frameworks (such as ASP and SharePoint) and social networks (Yammer and others), Microsoft is also doing its bit to empower B2B marketers to engage audiences.

Apple, in turn, not only made pretty devices that we can use to access the web, it's also created a very clever closed marketplace that has profound implications for push messaging – the type of marketing that enables us to reach interested, committed prospects.

These companies – and many others – help digitally savvy B2B marketers make sales and turn pixels into profit every day. The way we're embracing these businesses and integrating them into our lives prompted IT research giant Gartner to predict that by 2017, the chief marketing officer will have a bigger IT budget than the CIO.

BY 2017, THE CHIEF MARKETING OFFICER WILL HAVE A BIGGER IT BUDGET THAN THE CIO

Later in this chapter we'll look at the tactics you can use in order to take full advantage of the opportunities these technology-led monoliths can give you. We'll also shed some light on SEO (the process of getting Google to love you), how to build websites that deliver a great user experience, and on showcasing information in a manner that will have the highest possible impact. Then we'll look at other activities and tools, such as marketing automation, that'll help you stand out in a very congested world.

But before we get to the nitty-gritty of how to haul in buyers who are poised to make a buying decision, let's unpack the three big challenges facing B2B marketers in the digital age: visibility, accessibility and credibility, or VAC.

THREE DIGITAL CHALLENGES

Visible, accessible and credible – or how to stand out

The difference between companies who are successful at harnessing the internet to build profitable sales and those who aren't comes down to three simple things: making sure they get found, making sure their message comes across clearly and making sure that message is credible. This boils down to being visible, accessible and credible (VAC), because we all know the internet is full of lies, distortions and half-truths.

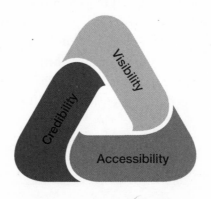

Visibility

The internet is like the proverbial huge haystack in which you are trying to find that elusive needle. Somewhere in the region of 42 trillion pages of information are clamouring for attention, so it's not easy to find any needle – unless you have an awful lot of time on your hands or a very powerful magnet.

Buying decision makers don't have much time – and even fewer will have magnets. So you need to work doubly hard to get your message into the right place at the right time. This means you need to be really easy to find (and use some clever techniques in the process). In short, if you want your needle to be discovered in the internet haystack, it needs to be very big and very magnetic.

THE INTERNET CONSISTS OF AROUND 42 TRILLION PAGES

Accessibility

Chances are you have a laptop, a desktop, a smartphone and, possibly, a tablet.

The prospect accessing your content via LinkedIn on an iPad wants a very different experience to the decision maker who's poring over product specs on your website from his desktop.

Dozens of devices with varying screen sizes and heaps of channels require you to have the skills of a shape-shifter to put your content into a format that'll have the impact you need. If you don't present your content in a form that makes your prospective customers' lives easy, they will desert you and head to a competitor who is attending to their needs.

Credibility

Because there is so much competition out there, digital content that generates sales by creating trust needs to be succinct, relevant to the audience's needs (and not your wants), and have a strong-enough call-to-action to bring a prospect into your buying cycle. This means your content must be credible: the audience who influences buying decisions needs to trust it.

It takes self-restraint to be relevant and credible. It's no good if you create content that is a thinly veiled sales pitch, because nobody will be interested. Customers don't want someone selling something to them.

It is far more important to get out there and see what your audience is worried about and what they need to achieve for themselves and for their business. So your mission should be to weave their concerns into content that educates, informs and enriches.

Get your VAC right, and you'll reap the benefits. You'll now be on the right track towards creating profitable sales. And you'll be able to see for yourself how well it's working. Get your VAC wrong, and your digital marketing is likely to be anonymous and naive. You'll be turned down if it's as VACANT as a government think-tank.

IT TAKES SELF-RESTRAINT TO BE RELEVANT AND CREDIBLE

Metrics – using data to know your prospects and predict their behaviour

In Chapter 8 (Marketing united), we said that the sole purpose of marketing is to attract and retain profitable customers.

The advent of the internet – and how it has altered customer behaviour in the buying cycle – makes it essential to connect with prospects digitally and to build long-term relationships with buying decision makers.

Tech companies have made it easier for us to access the internet and to use it to our advantage to position and promote content that captures your market's attention and motivates them to find out more.

The next step now is how to understand what getting your customers' attention means. There are two fundamental aspects of digital marketing that differentiate it from traditional marketing: segmentation and measurement.

Segment, segment and segment some more

Even if you have limited know-how, it is possible to profile your audience. You might not know who they are, but by using analytics and measurement tools you will be able to see where they are, how they're engaging with you, what content they are reading, how they're responding to it, and how they're sharing this with their peer group.

This data allows us to put our different audiences into categories, making it easier for us to reach them with content that will motivate them to buy because it is credible and relevant to their specific concerns and requirements.

This impact can be measured. John Wanamaker, the doyen of 19th- and early 20th-century retail, is credited with the line, 'Half of the money I spend on advertising is wasted; the trouble is I don't know which half.' Sadly, he missed the digital age.

Each blog post you write, and each social media comment you post, can be monitored to check its level of engagement.

Ongoing measurement allows you to repeat campaigns, so that you can focus your effort on tactics that deliver value and attain outcomes. This enables you to divert your marketing spend from activities that don't deliver the results you want to those that do.

There are some amazing tools out there that can help you on your journey of getting to know your customers and their behaviour. Google Analytics ought to be at the top of any digital marketers' list of bookmarks. It's free, and it's packed with incredible insights. And it's not difficult to use. If you spend only half an hour playing around with it, you'll get to see how people arrive at your website, where they are based, what they are looking at (and how long they look at it for). You'll be able to follow their user journey as they navigate through site pages. And if you set up goals, you can check how many did what you wanted, while you're also able to see where people fell out of the buying cycle.

TACTICAL MARKETING – PUSHING THE PIXEL

Up to now we've looked at why you should be putting digital at the centre of your marketing strategy. You've also seen that its impact can be analysed, helping you do your job even more effectively.

Now it's time to get under the hood of this machine called tactical marketing. This section focuses on tactics and provides some guidance on how to use them.

B2B marketers can harness the internet in many ways to discover, connect and convert prospects. What follows is therefore not a conclusive list but a selection of high-impact focus areas that'll turbo-charge your marketing efforts.

You'll be likely to use each of these tactics at different stages during your customers' digital interactions with you.

Creating results through actions

We usually avoid jargony acronyms, but here we've coined one to help you remember the different stages of securing new customers: *cream*, which stands for *create*, *reach*, *engage*, *acquire* and *maintain*. It captures the essence of what you need to do if you're to differentiate yourself and get prospective clients to buy your product or service, instead of your competitors' products or services. Perhaps you also have a childhood memory of milk in glass bottles with *cream* that had floated to the top – the best part!

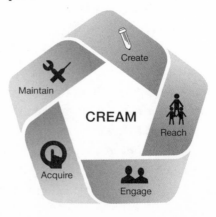

Create your platforms and content

Let's begin with creating your environment and your content. Without these, you won't be able to reach, engage, acquire or maintain your prospects and clients.

Platform one – your digital kingdom

Everything starts with your website. Unlike some of the other platforms out there (for example, social media), this is your space. You own it. It's a place where you share your brand story, connect people directly to your company and, more importantly, create that critical first impression. It's your *digital kingdom.*

You wouldn't turn up for a meeting with a key prospect in a dirty T-shirt and a ripped pair of jeans and then proceed to ramble through a disjointed presentation. In the same way as you attend to your personal attire, you need to put on your best digital wardrobe.

A good place to begin is with your website's user experience. Your site serves one single purpose: to expose people to your proposition and to elicit an action from them. This means you have to put time and effort into mapping out the customer journey – on a content map, which we looked at in Chapter 5 – and building a clear and coherent design that allows users to find information quickly and intuitively. If you don't, they'll drop you and move off to your competitor's better-thought-through platform.

Your site's architecture (putting content into folders by topic, making sure URLs are consistent) will help people find the right stuff. It also helps search engines classify and surface your content, something that is pretty important, as you'll find out shortly.

Ensure that your site is *mobile friendly*. Business decision makers aren't always sitting behind their desks when they conduct their research. In fact, the advent of second screens means they're equally likely to be browsing their tablet in the evening or checking stuff on their cellphone in the airport departure lounge. A study by *Forbes* magazine found that 25 per cent of executives have purchased a product or service for their business via mobile channels. That's why you need to make sure that the content you've invested time and energy creating delivers the best possible impression.

---

25 PER CENT OF EXECUTIVES HAVE PURCHASED A PRODUCT OR SERVICE FOR THEIR BUSINESS VIA MOBILE

While people have been talking about responsive web design for years (this is the process that scales your site to work across all devices), the move towards responsiveness gained momentum in 2015, when Google released an algorithm update to prioritise mobile-friendly sites in mobile search.

And when we explore tactics in terms of *reach*, you'll discover that search engines need to be your best friends.

Andy Zimmerman, chief marketing officer at Evergage, a consultancy that helps businesses create personalised content, complains that websites often fail to engage prospects because all visitors are treated the same way and are shown the same information.

He suggests that a website should build out navigation and content based on how a person arrives on your site and what they look at, dynamically serving up the most relevant content based on their needs. Marketing automation – one of the tactics covered later in this chapter – will shed some light on how to do this.

Social does belong at work
We've now covered some of the basics in building a website. You're not finished building, though, as you'll need to cover your *social media platforms* – and yes, these do belong in a B2B environment, provided you do social properly.

In the section on engaging your prospects, we'll look at how you can use social media to communicate with your audience – but before you do that, you need to create your presence. Here, some words of caution are in order: don't be fooled into believing that social is your own environment. Unlike your website, it's not.

LinkedIn, Twitter and Facebook own the data on their sites – they are merely providing a marketplace in which you can open dialogue with their customers. This makes it tremendously important for you to take people from your social platform to your owned platform (your website).

If you decide to jump into social media, do so properly and build a platform that is customised to your business and mirrors your branding. Each of the major platforms will allow you to incorporate varying degrees of your own corporate identity, so follow their guidance carefully.

App-lying yourself

Something else you might consider building is an app. Apps are popular. In fact, they're beyond popular.

In June 2015, Apple announced that in only seven years since the launch of its App Store, there had been over 100 billion app downloads. While most of these were games and consumer-driven apps, many – such as Evernote and Dropbox – were developed for a B2B audience and are used by companies to maintain relationships with customers.

So, if it's appropriate – if it adds to your customers' success – build your own app. For example, your app could be one that enables your sales team and your customers to check on the status of orders. However, don't create an app for the sake of it.

Creating clever content

We already mentioned the platforms you can build to engage your audience. Now we come to the most important part: *effective content*. With your site's structure and design in place, your attention should shift to words and pictures.

Good content is punchy. It distils your points of difference and encourages people to respond (remember content marketing in Chapter 5?).

A tried and tested piece of advice that is given to many a junior journalist is to assume your audience has the mental capacity and understanding of a nine-year-old child. While this doesn't mean you should assume your readers are dunces, it does mean you need to simplify your content. Dan Roth, one of LinkedIn's executives, states that 'if your content isn't driving conversation, you're doing it wrong'.

Once you've handled your core product and service information, you need to focus on creating a constant stream of new content. The best, cheapest and most effective way of doing this is by means of a *blog*. According to HubSpot, marketers who prioritise blogging are 13 times more likely to see a positive return on investment than those who don't. The same organisation's research found that businesses with large websites (400+ pages) get six times more leads than companies with 50 to 100 pages. So, create a blog schedule that'll add insight to your core products and services. Don't make excuses if your team doesn't have the aptitude or capacity to write. Hire a professional: there are many ex-journalists and professional writers out there who'd give their eye teeth for a retainer.

Remember that good content is also visual. Complex messages can be simplified by conveying them in the form of infographics, factoids, memes, decision trees and guides.

Some final words on content: in the section on VAC in this chapter, we emphasised the need for credibility. You also need *actionability*. Step back to Chapter 5's B2B content map for a reminder on the importance of your CTAs (calls-to-action). Your content needs them.

MARKETERS WHO PRIORITISE BLOGGING
ARE 13 TIMES MORE LIKELY TO SEE A
POSITIVE RETURN ON INVESTMENT
THAN THOSE WHO DON'T

Reach your audience

In the movie *Field of Dreams*, Kevin Costner's character is walking through his cornfield when a voice out of nowhere says: 'If you build it, he will come.' In other words, just do it and you'll get a result. Sadly for you, that ain't going to happen in today's digital world. No matter how much effort you put into your new website, if you don't promote it, people simply won't find it.

With somewhere in the region of a billion websites and trillions of web pages out there, the only way to prevent yours becoming obsolete is to reach out to your audience and pull them in. There are many high-impact *digital tactics* you can use to expose your brand to an online audience. We'll focus on three of these in this section: SEO, paid advertising and online PR.

Search engine optimisation (SEO) – digital gold dust

People who visit your site based on an organic search (the listings below the adverts) are far more committed and engaged than those who arrive from other channels.

Search Engine Journal, the search-engine optimisation industry's bible, reports that SEO leads have a much better chance of turning into sales – a 14.6 per cent close rate, which compares rather favourably with print advertising and direct mail, which average 1.7 per cent.

As we saw in Chapter 9, gaining a third-party endorsement (in this case the media) helps influence prospective buyers. There is no better endorsement that your website is credible than the one that Google and other search engines give when they display you at the top of their search-engine results pages. But if you want some of this gold dust, beware: SEO is a technical game, with plenty of snake oil being peddled to the unwary.

Understandably, getting to the top of a search engine's 'free' listings is not easy. If it were, we'd all be up there. Google is said to look at over 200 ranking factors. While this means there are plenty of nuances, there are three distinct things that will affect your ability to appear on page one: your competition, your content and your credibility.

Your competition. There are only 10 places on the first page of a Google search-engine listing (and sometimes fewer). Few people click through to the second or third page. You may even know the SEO question-and-answer joke: Question: 'Where's the best place to hide a body?' – Answer: 'On page two of Google.' Even if the joke makes you groan, there's more than a grain of truth in it. If your competitors are investing in SEO and they've been doing it for some time, you'll have to be smarter than they are while also recognising that it will take time to get up there and join them.

Also bear in mind that competition may not be rivals with similar products and services. Instead, many may be on classifieds sites, news platforms or broader sources of online information (very often you'll see Wikipedia in the first few results of a search).

The content of your site. Search engines like websites that have lots of quality content that is relevant to your target market and that update their content frequently. This indicates to them that you're likely to be a good source of information and will potentially answer their users' questions. Remember that search engines stay in business only if they're able to provide great answers to questions.

As part of their content evaluation, search engines also look at the architecture of your site and its technical markup, so you need to make sure your digital team is familiar with metadata, H tags, alt attributes, robots.txt and .htaccess files. This sounds complex, and much of it is – in fact, it's really complex.

So how do you make your site relevant? By understanding the language your audience talks. Chances are that this language is not the feature-rich acronym-laden language spoken in your boardroom. A tip is to use the free keyword research tool in Google's AdWords program to help you. It will help you see the keywords people type in when they're looking for products or services like yours. Once you've got a list of these, incorporate them into your content.

Then there are lots of website plugins that help build these phrases into some of the important technical areas that search engines look at (such as your page titles and meta descriptions). Yoast is a good one if you're running a WordPress website.

The credibility of your site. Many factors influence a search engine's perception of your site's quality. Remember the 200-odd elements mentioned earlier? Some of them include the number, relevance and authority of other sites that link to you, the number of times your brand is mentioned in online conversations (press coverage, social media and so on), the age of your domain and the interactions people have when they visit your site.

Building credibility means you need to incorporate an SEO-first mindset into all your other marketing activities. Include links back to your site in your press releases. Create great content that other websites will naturally want to link to. If you're in the business of supplying solar power systems, a good example would be to create a calculator that allows businesses to see how much power they use. This will help your users understand what to buy, and chances are that this will encourage other websites covering the topic to link back to your calculator.

Building credibility also means providing your audience with engaging content. We'll look at ways of measuring engagement in the section on measuring success shortly.

Paying for position

If you can't rank organically, start advertising. According to PwC, global internet advertising spend will grow from US$135 billion in 2014 to US$240 billion by 2019, so you'll be in good company.

But be careful: while online advertising is a great way to drive traffic, it can hit you with a double whammy. If campaigns aren't managed effectively, costs can run away as leads fail to materialise.

There are two distinct types of ads:

Display or banner ads are similar to conventional print advertising, except that people can click on the ad and be guided to your website, making it easier to measure the campaign's success. Ads are typically bought on a pay-per-click basis or through a CPM model (where costs are based on the number of times people see the ad). However, as these ads tend to target customers who are not actively looking for a product, they are best used if your goal is to build awareness rather than clinch immediate sales. To set up a display advertising campaign you can either approach publishers directly or advertise through Google's display network (a collection of websites that make inventory available to Google).

Text ads, like the ones you usually see on Google's or Bing's search return pages, target customers who are actually looking for something specific. These operate on an auction basis, with the companies that are willing to bid the most getting top billing for their ads. The best way to minimise cost and improve clickthrough rates is by using keywords that are most closely aligned to the products and services on your website. Look out for terms like 'exact match', 'broad match modifier' and 'negative keywords' when you set up your campaign. Using these will help you target your ads at the *right* audience.

If you use the internet regularly, you may have noticed that after you visit a website, you constantly see their ads appearing everywhere you go.

These companies are using a crafty technique called remarketing. This is a process through which search engines such as Google capture your cookie data (your PC's unique 'fingerprint') and then target you specifically by showing ads for products they 'know' you're interested in.

If you are on the receiving end of remarketing, it can be frustrating (particularly if you've visited a website you shouldn't have), but the technique has proved to deliver excellent results.

Online PR: building your digital reputation

While we covered the importance of PR in Chapter 9 (PR and B2B: the perfect couple), don't for a moment think that PR is confined to the traditional world of print media relations and event management.

The plethora of blogs and the insatiable appetite online news portals have for content means the internet must become an integral part of every public relations plan. There are three clear reasons for this:

- It can help your *SEO*. Sites that write about you might link to you. Even if they don't, the fact that your brand name appears online delivers citation value in the eyes of a search engine. So if you're sending press releases to bloggers and the media at large, write keyword-optimised copy and include links back to your site.

- The internet's full of *niches*. While some of these are dark corners you might not want to find yourself in, there are special-interest websites for everything – far more so than in the traditional print world. You've probably discovered a few yourself. So regardless of how obscure your product or service, you'll find someone who's interested in it online, and who'll be only too happy to hear from you.

- The internet *generates leads*. If a site has a good review of your product or service, chances are that people will click through to your site when there's a link. And if there isn't one, it's easy for them to open a new tab and search for your business. It's much harder to 'click through' from a newspaper!

Engage your prospects

In the last few sections you've found ways for building your platforms and getting people to visit them. Now you need to convince them to stick around. So let's look at some tactics you can deploy to encourage prospects to hang around and come back for more.

Two of the best engagement tactics are social media and email marketing. But before we tackle those, let's go back to your website, which should be the hub of all your activity.

You ought to have spotted that the best way of creating engagement is to couple great content with an effective website architecture that makes it easy to access. But in order to create true engagement, you want to put a name and a face to the person sitting behind the PC. So make sure you've got calls-to-action (CTAs) and conversion points across your site and all related marketing collateral. This can be as simple as asking someone to provide an email address to access a white paper or a detailed case study.

Getting chatty: being social for business's sake

Social media are a confusing concept for B2B marketers, as their very name implies that they are more about fun than work. However, social media are essential to your organisation's survival in the competitive B2B market. In fact, a recent Content Marketing Institute study found that 92 per cent of B2B marketers use social media not only to engage their customers, but also to actively drive sales.

To engage well in social media, you need to remain relevant. By understanding how you are relevant to your audience's needs, you will keep your subscribers loyal and encourage them to share content, bringing more prospects into the buying cycle.

Something that we touched upon in the section on creating your platforms is that one challenge of social media is that you don't own the platform, so if you want to own the customer, you need to use their playground (be it LinkedIn, Twitter or Facebook) to guide them to your website.

The various channels can each play a role in reaching prospects and engaging customers, but the channel you use will depend on your business requirements. Many B2B organisations rely on Facebook as a staff recruitment and retention channel. Others use it to build brand awareness. Few use it in the process of creating sales. LinkedIn and Twitter are more effective at this.

If your goal is to share the more technical aspects of your business with fellow professionals, LinkedIn offers opportunities to create a page or join a group related to the topics you discuss. If you want to invest in visual content, YouTube may provide a better platform. General Electric is one company that has done this to great effect.

It's all in the timing

Regardless of your social objectives, having an informed social media calendar is key to distributing meaningful messages to your audience at the right time. A good calendar might focus on issues relevant to your business (such as new product launches). It will also incorporate broader events and news agendas.

While a strong social media presence across all your channels should display value to your customers, you need to get the customers there in the first place.

If they're not finding you organically (stumbling across you or being channelled through their friends and contacts), you may want to increase your visibility by promoting social media posts through the various advertising opportunities offered by Facebook, LinkedIn and Twitter.

Getting ahead of the competition

Social media can also play a pivotal role in helping you see what your competitors are up to. Social listening tools such as Radian6 allow you to monitor the information your competitors share with their followers. By shining your spotlight on their social media activities you will be able to understand what information they're highlighting, see what causes real engagement and measure how your performance compares to theirs.

Email marketing for high performance

In 2009, the *Wall Street Journal* published an article claiming that email was dead. Ironically, it was the most emailed article of the day. By 2015, email had become such an entrenched part of the B2B marketer's toolkit that a study conducted by Salesforce found that 73 per cent of businesses felt it was core to their business. Companies think this because there is quantifiable evidence that sending emails to qualified, opted-in prospects is the most effective method of converting interest to sales. If you're getting into email marketing, here are a few quick tips:

- Build an effective list. You've probably got one already. If not, you should build one. The best way of doing this is to let people read quality information on your website and then encourage them to sign up to a mailing list.
- Get the creative side of things in order: a quality HTML message has a far better ROI than a simple text-based one. Use images sparingly, and make sure they're small so that they will download quickly.
- Write pithy copy – it's that simple.
- Work on your call-to-action (CTA). Ideally, make the CTA stand out by using colours or a button, so readers know what's expected of them. If appropriate, create defined landing pages for each email campaign. If you're pushing a new product, instead of sending the recipient to the product listing page, you might want to direct them to a special page on your website where they can find the relevant product *data* and broader information on industry trends that supports why customers need your product.
- Include your contact details and build an *unsubscribe* link into the footer.
- Then segment your messages. Personalised messages that relate to people's specific interests and needs are far more likely to appeal than mass communications.
- Do split testing. If you're sending out an email about a new product, divide the mailing into various groups. Send each segment a slight variation on the original message. Consider changing the copy, or amend the subject line, as this will help you pinpoint the most effective way of communicating.
- Test and optimise. Don't make the mistake of thinking your email will look the same in all browsers. Something that looks fine in Outlook is likely to break in Gmail.
- Measure and repeat. After a few mailings you ought to see some patterns emerge. An analysis of the bounce rate, the opens and the clickthroughs will give you the data you need to optimise future mailings.

Acquire business

By now you should have created a great platform with compelling content, reached out to your prospects and engaged them. The penultimate element of an effective digital marketing strategy is *acquisition* – or turning interest into sales.

There are many ways to manage prospective clients and to take them from an early interest in your product to the point at which they sign on the dotted line.

Platforms such as Salesforce are a boon to online and offline marketers, as they help you manage prospects, by focusing on those with the highest propensity to convert. But there's one tech tool that absolutely rocks in the digital activation arena: marketing automation.

Letting it do it itself

As its name suggests, *marketing automation* does heaps of work by itself. In the section on creating your platforms we heard of Andy Zimmerman at Evergage, who spoke of the need to personalise content and messages to your audience.

Marketing automation software allows you to do this by profiling and segmenting your audience's activities when they engage with your content. SharpSpring and HubSpot are products that allow you to visualise which channels drive visitors to your website and analyse the content they're reading.

Scarily, they also capture your cookie data and IP details, so each time you visit a site that's being tracked, your behaviour profile is extended (this, of course, is handy if *you* are using them). While a profile is not worth much if they don't know who you are, maybe you'll fall for one of their neat CTAs and put your name and contact details into a form.

This is when marketing automation changes into something akin to the philosopher's stone, and B2B marketers can start engaging in acquisition alchemy.

FOR B2B MARKETERS, MARKETING AUTOMATION IS AKIN TO ACQUISITION ALCHEMY

Let's revisit Zimmerman's vision of the future. He wants to serve content to people based on their consumption behaviour. With the correct configuration, marketing automation will start sending your prospects emails containing content it reckons they'll be interested in. It can dynamically display articles on your website, showing people content that is aligned to their interests (and, with true stealth, it can tweak CTAs until it finds the perfect line to hook your prospect).

Think about it: you can deliver timely and relevant content to prospects based on what their history suggests they want to read. It's scary. But it's real. And it delivers acquisitions, by the bucketload.

Measure success

We'll get to measurement in Chapter 11 (Measuring the king), but because everything can be tracked in the online world, it's such an important topic that it merits some attention in this chapter.

As everyone is probably well aware, in this brave, scary world, every time we send an email, access the internet or WhatsApp a friend, our actions are captured. Huge amounts of data are stored. Some of this information is used for nefarious purposes, but it can give marketers tremendous insights into where, how and why people respond (or don't) to their marketing campaigns. The amount of information available to you can seem daunting, but used correctly, it'll empower you to start making data-based decisions that enable you to analyse, interpret and repeat your online activity.

Big (or any) data analysis

Einstein's definition of insanity was to do the same thing over and over, while expecting a different result. One of the greatest attributes of digital media is that you can do something and analyse it in real time, tweaking and changing your tactics on the fly to emphasise what works best.

The starting point in data analysis is defining meaningful goals, followed by setting comparative baselines so you can measure changes in activity.

Whether you're looking at the results of email split testing, understanding why some social media posts deliver better engagement than others, studying which AdWords campaigns deliver the most leads or gauging why your competitors continue to outrank you in Google, there's a wealth of tools you can use to interpret which parts of your digital marketing toolkit are generating the most significant results. The most user-friendly tool is the free one Google offers all website owners: Google Analytics. To turbo-boost your marketing performance, you ought to spend a similar amount of time analysing your activity as you put into its initial implementation. Google Analytics has a pretty simple tutorial, so study it. (If you're brave, you can even take the exam, which isn't a typical Department-of-Education-30-per-cent-pass story: you need to get 80 per cent. And that's a good thing, because if you're going to work with data, you need to know what you're doing.)

WHAT'S COMING DOWN THE PIPE?

Google has only been around since 1998, Facebook since 2004 and Twitter since 2006. They're veritable youngsters in comparison to B2B giants such as John Deere and General Electric, which were founded in 1837 and 1892, respectively. However, the speed with which these newbies have been able to dominate the digital landscape illustrates just how rapidly the online world moves.

And this really ought to prompt B2B marketers to ask themselves what's coming down the funnel that could impede or improve the way they interact with customers in future. Here are a few predictions.

Immersive reality

Imagine a scenario in which there's no need to send a salesperson out to pitch your product. Screen-sharing services such as GoToMeeting take on a whole new dimension, enabling you to give your prospects an all-singing-and-dancing demo in a virtual world.

Granted, this might still be a bit out there, but with the advent of augmented reality (AR), it won't be long before businesses start finding ways to harness tools such as Oculus Rift to deeply immerse their prospects into their propositions by delivering virtual 'in-person' demos.

AR is here, and with the investment that Google and others are making in bridging the gap between 'real real' and 'virtual real', it's only a matter of time before this technology becomes commercially viable and ends up in a boardroom like yours.

Anonymity

Across the world, governments are stepping up privacy legislation. Right now it is focused on protection of data and opt-out marketing. Much of this makes sense: if you weren't aware of remarketing or marketing automation until you read about these techniques in the previous section, you probably felt a shiver running down your spine. After all, none of us enjoy receiving unsolicited information, and increasingly we want to be in control of the news we receive.

In 2014, Google was required to implement European legislation concerning the 'right to be forgotten'. This compelled publishers to redact or remove negative commentary. Chances are high that the move towards anonymity will continue gaining momentum and empower audiences to choose what they want and don't want to hear from others.

But for now, you don't need to let what might happen in the future prevent you from utilising it in the present.

The internet of things

No look into the future, however brief, would be replete without mention of the internet of things: a world where our fridges order milk and our watches alert doctors to impending medical conditions.

While the connected world of wearable technology and internet-enabled devices is widely spoken about in a consumer context, it presents tremendous opportunities for B2B marketers. By 2020, the number of devices connected to the internet is expected to exceed 40 billion. General Electric reckons that the 'industrial internet' will add US$10 to US$15 trillion to global GDP over the next twenty years.

Aside from helping personalise marketing, distribute real-time messages and track buyer journeys (something we already get from marketing automation), the internet of things will give us real insights into product usage, and help marketers understand how and when customers use their products. This will provide meaningful insights that'll help us adapt products to meet customer preferences – insights that will help create sales, protect margins and build market share.

DIRECTIONS TO RESULTS

The internet is the B2B marketer's best friend, and your ability to see what's working (and what's not) gives you an opportunity to optimise your performance.

Directions to results for Chapter 10 will show you how to:
- *use digital technology to create lasting engagement with your audience*
- *talk to your audiences in their language*
- *analyse your competitors' strengths and weaknesses, so that you can compensate for the former and outperform on the latter*
- *see who your buying decision maker really is*
- *measure campaign outcomes to improve conversion.*

Follow these steps to get into the fast lane:
- All the different digital programs you use have dashboards that track audience engagement. Are you using them effectively? From Google Analytics to AdWords and Hootsuite to Mail-Chimp, you have the power. Are you applying it?
- Understand the language your audience uses when they're searching for products or services similar to yours. If you have a Google account (which is as simple as setting up a Gmail address), log into AdWords, open up the keyword planner tool and type in a few keywords. Which ones have the highest search volumes? Are you using these phrases in your marketing material? If not, do so.
- Baseline your website's visibility against your competitors. Where do you rank on your top keywords? Use tools such as Screaming Frog to check how your competitors have optimised their sites, and work with Majestic SEO to understand your competitors' strengths and weaknesses, and to find out where they're getting their backlinks from. Can you spot the gaps and make a plan?

- Create a content calendar and map this calendar out to cover the various digital tactics you're using. A regular schedule for blog posts, email newsletters and social media posts based on topics that interest your audience will give you more credibility in the battle for engagement.
- Think about the key metrics you want to measure and log in to Google Analytics to set up goals. Such goals could be to measure the number of downloads or contact-form submissions you get.
- Are you doing the same thing over and over? Is it working? Could it work better? If you don't know, test it. Tweak your email subject lines and content, and run split tests to see which one performs better. Change your website landing pages, move CTAs around, and log into Google Analytics to see the difference.

11

Measuring the king:
ROI and how to get it

WHY MEASURE, WHAT TO MEASURE, HOW TO MEASURE

Coming up in this chapter:
- Measuring marketing performance: set the right expectations
  - Sales and margins: your performance benchmarks
  - Measuring the route to profitable sales
- Why measure?
- What to measure and how to measure it
  - Measuring value performance
  - Measuring content performance
  - Measuring channel performance
  - Measuring lead generation performance
  - Measuring conversion performance
  - Customer retention performance
- Alignment: measurement through agreement
  - Why alignment matters
  - Results through alignment
  - Improvement through measurement
- Why *Le ROI* is king: measuring return on marketing spend
  - Setting targets and measuring progress towards them
- Measuring with muscle
  - Some things may need to change
- Measuring with purpose
  - Make sure it matters
- Measuring market share

MEASURING MARKETING PERFORMANCE: SET THE RIGHT EXPECTATIONS

By changing your expectations of marketing's purpose, you'll change how you measure and improve its performance.

The purpose of marketing clearly is to attract and retain profitable customers. So sales and margins are *the* benchmarks for measuring your performance.

To improve the direct contribution of your marketing efforts to profitable sales, you need to measure that contribution from start to finish.

Sales and margins: your performance benchmarks

Here are the results you can expect to achieve through measurement:
- accelerate customers from 'I'm just browsing' to 'Where do I sign?'
- predict the probability of converting leads to profitable sales – i.e. forecasting revenues and profits
- identify where you're getting the most bang for your marketing buck – and where you aren't
- highlight how well customers' needs are understood and what must be improved to meet them.

If you want to put a smile on your CEO's dial, this is the sort of talk you need to walk.

Measuring the route to profitable sales

The big marketing objectives of brand awareness, product positioning, customer insight, lead generation, lead nurturing and customer engagement are the very stuff of marketing. But if you can't measure their contribution to profitable sales, they're nothing but empty buzzphrases.

Naturally, commercially focused marketers want the big objectives to deliver the goal – profitable sales.

We know that customers have to be aware of your brand before they can even consider buying from you. But awareness doesn't automatically mean they will buy. And if they do buy, are they buying at an acceptable margin?

We also know that leads need to be generated and managed before they can be converted to revenue and profits. But generating leads doesn't automatically mean you are generating profitable sales.

The point here is that there has to be a direct link between the objectives and the goal. The important word is *direct*. So, what *direct* contributions are your marketing activities making to sales and margins? The *only* way to answer this question is to measure these contributions.

WHY MEASURE?

Why do we measure? Because measurement empowers improvement.

> *Measurement is the first step that leads to control and eventually to improvement. If you can't measure something, you can't understand it. If you can't understand it, you can't control it. If you can't control it, you can't improve it.*
> — Dr H. James Harrington, CEO,
> Harrington Group International

Dr James Harrington has long been regarded as a world authority on improving business performance. It is worth looking into his statement that 'measurement is the first step that leads to control and eventually to improvement' – in other words, if you want improvement, you need to measure first.

MEASUREMENT EMPOWERS IMPROVEMENT

Measurement is enlightenment; it should be the happy light that guides your marketing into the future, rather than an autopsy of the gory past. Measurement provides the framework to formulate and implement marketing activities that are linked to profitable sales. It should not be an afterthought that gets tagged on to the end of your activities. As a marketing management function, measurement isn't about justification: measurement is about motivation.

Measurement should be the engine that drives and supports your decisions on how to generate profitable sales.

MEASUREMENT IS THE ENGINE
THAT DRIVES PROFITABLE SALES

WHAT TO MEASURE AND HOW TO MEASURE IT

Measuring value performance

> *We tend to overvalue the things we can measure and undervalue the things we cannot.*
>
> – John Hayes, CMO, American Express

If you can measure what customers value, you'll understand what motivates them to buy. This means you'll understand what creates your sales and protects your margins.

We emphasised how critically important it is to understand what customers value in Chapter 3 (B2B's Big Five buying motivators). A vital lesson was that value is not a soft issue: it is tangible, it can be defined and it can be measured.

Value can be defined through its component parts: response, service, time, quality and price. These are the five factors of value. The value created by your products and services can be measured using the value analysis process we looked at in Chapter 4 (Working with buying motivators).

In a nutshell, these two chapters deal with this blunt fact: above all else, you first have to develop crystal-clear insights into what customers *value* before you can generate profitable sales. You have to measure value in order to understand it, control it and improve it.

How to measure value performance

We dealt with value performance in Chapter 4. In summary, measuring value performance requires you to listen: listen to your customers; listen to everyone in your overall market that influences buying decisions; listen to *how* you build their success. Listening – and reading between the lines – is the basis for discovering all the ways your products or services create value. Remember King Richard and his horse from Chapter 3 and that customers don't always say clearly what they want?

We saw in Chapter 8 (Marketing united) that anyone who affects the customer experience should be routinely providing feedback to a couple of key customer-centric questions (refer back to the reality-check list you drew up at the end of Chapter 8 here):

- Where do we meet your expectations?
- Where do we let you down?

A continuing dialogue with customers reveals where they think you are providing too much value (over-delivering) and where they believe you are providing too little value (under-delivering). In Chapter 4, we also looked at how over-delivery and under-delivery create the value gap that causes all the problems associated with price.

So before you attempt to measure anything else, make sure you measure your value performance.

Measuring content performance

In Chapter 5 (Content is king!) we looked at how to create credible content that is relevant for each phase of the buying cycle.

It's imperative that you understand how your content moves buyers through the cycle – from showing initial interest to signing on the dotted line.

Content performance: what to measure

Here are the key questions you need to ask in order to measure content performance:

1. What type of content is generating interest?
2. Where is that content positioned in the buying cycle?
3. Out of all the people in your spheres of influence you looked at in Chapter 1, who is interested in the content?
4. Why are they interested – that is, how is your content relevant to them?
5. How significant is their influence on buying decisions?
6. What actions are being prompted by their interest?
7. How is your content moving them to the next phase? How is it keeping them in the cycle?
8. And, most importantly: Does your content result in a profitable, long-life sale?

The table that follows shows you how you might start measuring the effectiveness of your content, based on the questions listed above. To use the table, choose an item of content and begin to link it with the answers you need. The types of content used in this example are a white paper on industry trends and an insight article on product applications.

Response to content							
Type of content	Position of prospect within cycle?	Who is interested?	Why are they interested?	What is their level of influence?	Actions prompted?	Moved to next phase?	Profitable sales achieved?
White paper							
Insight article							
How is all this information recorded?							

As much of your content is likely to be online, you have an array of amazing tools you can use to measure performance to see how many reads, shares and downloads you get.

Many of these tools – like Google Analytics, which we touched on in Chapter 10 (Digital, digital, digital) – are free. Others come bundled with the software you might be using; the providers of your emailing program, for example, should be keen as mustard to show you their products are working.

But while they'll give you some of the information you need, tools alone aren't going to do the whole job for you. So what else do you need to do? Well, you need to record the right information, or else you won't have anything that's worth measuring!

So how do you record the right information? In Chapter 7 (Extra special delivery), we looked at *buyer personas* and the reasons why it's important to document who's who in the buying cycle. Let's look at these personas more closely now.

RECORD THE RIGHT INFORMATION TO HAVE SOMETHING THAT'S WORTH MEASURING

Keeping records: the importance of personas

A *persona* is a fact sheet on anyone in your spheres who influences buying decisions. It details who they are, what they do, the type of content that's relevant to them in the context of buying, and the channels that reach them best.

Personas record everything that relates to the buying behaviour of customers and prospects. They are the building blocks for creating relevant, credible content that motivates buying. How you generate that motivation brings us back to using measurement as a process to guide your marketing activities. All too often, activities are conceived of and implemented without the foggiest idea of how to measure response and record the results produced.

When analysing the performance of your content, it should be clear that calls-to-action (CTAs) are essential components of the measurement process: not only do CTAs have to be built into *all* your content right from the start, they also have to be structured in a way that captures the information you need, namely persona-based information.

CALLS-TO-ACTION (CTAS) ARE ESSENTIAL COMPONENTS OF THE MEASUREMENT PROCESS

In a digital-first world, it is relatively easy to include persona-based questions in a web form that prospects need to complete when they wish to download something or access valuable content.

But be aware that these forms might contain some lies. While some of the data captured will be accurate, not everything will be spot on. It's easy (and fun) for a junior clerk to tick the CEO checkbox when filling in a mandatory field on job function. So you'll need to do some offline validation to ensure the integrity of your information.

This highlights another reality: CTAs are not the only source for creating and maintaining personas. When you operate in a 'marketing united' environment, *all* internal direct contact with everyone who influences buying decisions has to be used as an information-gathering resource. Measurement-oriented questions need to be asked, and personas provide a formal, disciplined mechanism to capture the answers.

For example, at a live event you should ask visitors persona-related questions and ensure you have a way to capture the answers.

Here's a story to emphasise the point of record-keeping.

A company spends hundreds of thousands of bucks to showcase new products at a highly focused trade show. All visitor interactions are recorded in a red file kept in the 'staff only' room. In effect, the whole purpose of the show is distilled into that file, into a series of personas for both prospects and existing customers.

At the end of the show, the file is nowhere to be found. Lost? Or even worse, stolen? Measuring the value of that file falls into two parts: the known and billed costs of the show; and the potential sales and margins that were compromised. At the very minimum, a million bucks went missing that day.

Measuring channel performance

Don't count the people that you reach; reach the people who count.
                                                    – David Ogilvy

In Chapter 7 (Extra special delivery), we looked at how different channels produce different results as buyers progress through the buying cycle. As delivery mechanisms for your content, how effective is each channel in creating visibility across your overall market – in other words, are you reaching everyone who influences buying decisions?

You need to understand how effectively your channels move buyers to the point of purchase, from generating leads through to conversion into profitable sales.

Channel performance: what to measure

Here are the key questions you need to ask in order to measure channel performance:

1. Which channels are known to reach each of the audiences in your spheres of influence?
2. What are the links between channels and each phase in the buying cycle?
3. What actions are being prompted by each channel?
4. Which channels are moving customers towards profitable sales?

The table on the next page shows how you can link audiences to channels and the results they produce.

Response to content							
Type of content	Position of prospect within cycle?	Who is interested?	Why are they interested?	What is their level of influence?	Actions prompted?	Moved to next phase?	Profitable sales achieved?
Trade show							
Website							

Remember that you may want to segment the channels you use even further. How did a particular prospect land up at the trade show: did one of your colleagues invite him or her? Which digital tactic led the audience to your website and prompted an action? Was it SEO, an email or a social post?

Let's say your channels are doing a great job in terms of brand awareness. You're generating lots of interest during the first three phases of the cycle. You're highlighting industry needs and challenges, outlining the criteria to address them, and proposing specific solutions. You know this because of the volume of web traffic and type of downloads you're getting. In sales jargon, you're pumping loads of leads into the top of the funnel.

But is that interest moving prospects through to the next three phases? Is it leading to product demos or proof-of-concepts? Is that interest then generating requests for quotes and proposals? And are these then producing profitable sales? If leads aren't moving through the cycle, do you understand why not?

IF LEADS AREN'T MOVING THROUGH THE CYCLE, DO YOU UNDERSTAND WHY NOT?

One way to answer this question is by systematically recording channel performance on the personas of these leads. For example, a new product video might be getting loads of downloads, but do you know who's watching it and why? Do you know what they do and where they work? How significant is their influence on buying decisions? And do you know what their position is in the cycle? Are you even asking these questions? As Dr Harrington tells us: if you can't measure, you can't understand.

Measuring lead generation performance

By measuring the performance of your content and channels, you will understand *how* you are generating leads. To achieve your sales and profit goals, you now need to measure the *quality* and *quantity* of your leads. This process of measurement is typically known as 'lead scoring'.

How to measure lead quality

Obviously, you want to generate leads that have a high probability of converting to profitable sales. Such leads will have a number of characteristics that act as indicators of their quality. And by 'quality' we mean the likelihood of converting to sales.

Let's say the CEO, CFO and COO of a major player in a target market attend your live event. They talk through the benefits they are seeking. They like what you can provide and ask for a meeting to discuss pricing and lead times. The indicators suggest that this is a high-quality lead – one that, right now, looks likely to convert.

How you define your lead-quality indicators – and there may be dozens of them – is something we're going to look at in the next part of this chapter under the heading 'Alignment'. But before we go into this, here's a list of seven indicators you might want to measure in order to give your leads a score.

1. *Buying motivators* (response, service, time, quality and price): Product benefits need to be measured according to their significance on the buying decision and their significance to those who influence it. These rankings will show that, for example, a low price may be far less significant – far less valued – than a short lead time. Or bespoke integration may be irrelevant compared to 24/7 support services. These measurements will identify what will motivate the buying

decision of a prospect. And it means you will understand how to accelerate the likelihood of conversion by linking the right messages to the right people.

2. *Influence*: For each person involved in the buying decision, measure their level of authority and how committed they are to moving forward. This allows you to focus on securing the necessary authority and commitment to buy.

3. *Interactions*: You also need to measure the significance of various interactions with your market. A CEO attending a seminar might get a higher ranking than a senior technologist downloading a product sheet. But a senior technologist attending a product workshop at the CEO's request might rank highest of all. This quantifies the level of interest in making a buying decision.

Although not exactly measurements, the last four indicators are essential when ranking a lead's quality:

4. *Budget*: availability and likelihood of approval
5. *Time*: when the customer will buy and implement
6. *Price*: both revenue and profitability
7. *Fulfilment*: details of what steps need to be taken by your company and the customer in order to implement the solution being sought.

The last indicator (fulfilment) is particularly important, because it provides advance warning of what will be needed – and when – from production, stockholding, procurement, finance, sales and service, and distribution. It also highlights what needs to be done by the customer in order to implement a solution.

Fulfilment is always affected by changes in any of the other lead-quality metrics. For example, can you meet requests for faster implementation, or a larger order with bigger discounts, or modifications to a product? How do such changes affect the quality of the lead?

How to measure lead quantity

It is far easier to measure lead quantity than lead quality, because it's a simple counting game: How many leads are there in each phase of the cycle, and where did they come from? You already have an understanding of the source of your leads from measuring channel performance. So this type of measurement is simply a case of *numbers* and *positions*.

Numbers and positions matter, and here's why: let's say your measurements prove that all your leads are spread over phases 1 to 4, with a big zero in the others. This demonstrates that something is missing. Why aren't these leads confident enough to take the next step? What's holding them back? What needs to be done to get those leads moving forward? What needs to be done to *motivate* them to buy?

- Perhaps requirements are poorly understood or not being addressed with relevance and credibility. Are there concerns about product reliability, integration or availability?
- Maybe there are unresolved issues over maintenance and support. Is your price seen as uncompetitive, or even perhaps as too good to be true? Are you interacting with the prospect at too low a level?
- Measuring lead quantity in relation to the cycle prompts you to act upon the answers to these questions. This all boils down to measurement that directs improvement.

Counting leads within phases is the easy part. What's more difficult is to capture all your leads in one place. And that is something you absolutely have to do. Regardless of where they come from, all leads should pass through a single process. Here they get positioned in the cycle, become correctly qualified and are assigned appropriate *responses*. Speed and accuracy are the top priorities. So you will need to keep this process as slick and simple as possible.

Once you have processed a lead, what is the likelihood that this lead will convert? Out of all your leads, how do you identify the ones that will generate sales and margins? That's what you're going to look at next.

Measuring conversion performance

Conversion performance includes what is often referred to as 'lead nurturing'. This can be defined as communicating with customers in a way that is relevant and credible as they are 'nurtured' through the buying cycle.

Even though you may be generating high-quality leads, not all of them will convert to sales. Progress through the cycle can be derailed by circumstances in the economy, or in specific markets, or within the customer's organisation.

While there are events you can't control, you need to understand the ones you can control. This entails measuring the likelihood that a lead will convert to a profitable sale by giving it a conversion rating.

How to measure conversion rating

In the context of leads, the most vital statistic is the conversion rating (or CR).

The CR has the characteristics of a living thing. It changes as leads progress towards purchasing. On the next page is an example of how you might begin to measure CR using the lead-quality indicators of position, influence and budget.

	Position	Influence	Budget	CR %
Lead A	Phase 3 in cycle Attended trade show; not yet accepted seminar invite; incomplete persona	Unknown	Unknown	10%
Lead B	Phase 4 in cycle Downloaded product sheets; attended seminar; had product demo; complete persona; handed over to Sales	High COO is primary contact and chaired demo meeting; has sanction from IT, Operations and HR; internal resources in place; has budget authority; needs Finance approval	Proposal submitted; awaiting CFO approval and purchase order	90%
Lead C	Phase 5 in cycle Proposal submitted; multiple complete personas on all stakeholders	Necessary stakeholders agree to proceed; buying decision confirmed	Approved but subject to revised roll-out milestones set by overseas parent company	5%
	Question: *Where is all this information recorded?*			
	Answer: On the persona for each lead			

Here's why each lead is given the above CR values:

- **Lead A** gets a 10 per cent CR because the trade show attended was highly focused. Market sector and job function of this visitor both fit well with your lead-quality indicators. He wants to attend your next seminar and has an invitation. But could be only a tyre-kicker.
- **Lead B** merits a high CR of 90 per cent because all that is needed is a rubber stamp on your proposal when the CFO returns from leave.
- **Lead C** may look great, but your production team says they can't meet the revised roll-out milestones set by the customer's international head office. The CR was consequently downgraded to 5 per cent.

The purpose of an exercise like this is to:

- confirm the lead-quality indicators that combine to form the CR (more about this when we get to the subject of alignment)
- record the information for each of the personas involved in the lead.

How all this information is used brings you back, yet again, to the buying cycle. This time you will use the cycle as a framework to measure progress as leads move towards signing on the dotted line.

Measuring progress towards conversion

This measurement is fairly straightforward: a conversion rating shows you how likely it is that any given lead, at any given time, will convert to a profitable sale.

With its highly commercial focus, the CR forecasts:

- when sales will happen
- what revenues and profits those sales will generate
- what your company will need to do – operationally – to secure the revenues and profits.

Here, then, is how you might start to populate a CR chart. This example uses the same three leads we looked at earlier.

Phase 1 Identifying needs	Phase 2 Setting criteria	Phase 3 Specific research	Phase 4 Evaluation and testing	Phase 5 Selecting suppliers and negotiating	Phase 6 Buying and implementing
Lead A: CR = 10%					
Progress tracked on personas			Lead B: CR = 90%		
Progress tracked on personas				Lead C: CR = 5%	

Measuring CRs across the cycle also enables you to understand where you need to generate more leads (quantity) and the type (quality) of leads you need. Importantly, this example shows that the position of your leads in the cycle is no guarantee of a high CR.

The practice of allocating a CR to a lead based on the seven quality indicators listed earlier is a very important issue – and one that is typically handled badly or not at all. So you need to ensure that you make it crystal clear how your CR 'scoring' works. It also needs to be explained clearly to someone who is new to a structured approach to scoring and measurement.

The reason why this is so important is that an accurate CR – an accurate measurement – is the only mechanism that allows you to respond to leads in a motivating manner and drive the relationship forward to the point where a prospect will sign on the dotted line.

AN ACCURATE CR EMPOWERS YOU TO MOVE A PROSPECT TOWARDS SIGNING ON THE DOTTED LINE

Also bear in mind that the weighting given to each of the seven lead-quality indicators will vary from product to product and market to market. For example, if you're in the business of building rocket engines, a joint enquiry from NASA and the European Space Agency about a Mars journey might get a higher score than a similar enquiry from a maverick entrepreneur (or perhaps the same score, if the space-crazy maverick can prove that he's raised the necessary funds to fly to Mars!).

When measuring the CR, the key is to use all the quality indicators in order to arrive at a realistic score. As you do this, you'll become steadily more adept at assimilating all the relevant information and drawing a measured conclusion.

Note also that I am using the term *conversion rating* here, which differs widely from *lead scoring* and other similar terms. None of these other terms place such central importance on measuring the likelihood of a lead converting to a sale – and that's the only measurement that matters.

Once you have your processes in place for measuring leads and managing their progress towards profitable sales, you need to think about retaining customers.

Customer retention performance

In theory, customer retention should be easier in B2B markets than in B2C markets. It is much easier to switch to another toothpaste than to switch to a new ERP supplier, after all. However, losing a customer tends to be far more costly in B2B. That's why it is essential that customers stay customers.

The best way to retain customers is to ensure that your customers *continue* to recognise all the ways in which you contribute to their success. You do this by recognising how your products and services create value that motivates buying.

In terms of retention, the primary task is to reinforce and entrench those motivators through a continuous dialogue that pinpoints customers' needs and how to meet them. This dialogue helps you identify where you meet customers' expectations and create value – and where you don't.

In addition to measuring – and improving – your ongoing value performance, here's what you might also want to consider when assessing ways to strengthen customer retention:

- What is the potential to create more value by upselling and cross-selling?
- How easily could customers switch to a competitor?
- What are the reasons that would prompt them to switch?
- How likely is it that customers will recommend your products and services?

This last point is particularly important. We saw in Chapter 9 (PR and B2B: the perfect couple) that customer endorsements and recommendations are a vital component in the process of building sales and creating trust in your products and services.

Wherever possible, encourage customers to speak for you – to talk about all the ways in which you contribute to their success. Quote them in your content, promote them as speakers or guests at live events, introduce them to other customers, include them in presentations and best-practice white papers and, of course, feature them in case studies and social media posts.

Such endorsements are a powerful mechanism in customer retention. Every customer who endorses you is reinforcing – in their own mind – all the reasons why buying from you is the right choice.

EVERY CUSTOMER WHO ENDORSES YOU REINFORCES IN THEIR OWN MIND THE REASONS WHY BUYING FROM YOU IS THE RIGHT CHOICE

ALIGNMENT: MEASUREMENT THROUGH AGREEMENT

The buying cycle plays a critically important role in measuring and improving marketing performance. It lets you understand the type of content that's relevant to different people at different times. It builds your understanding of the channels that reach those people and when they reach them. It acts as the framework for measuring performance in lead generation and conversion. And it's a tool for forecasting revenue and profitability.

Within the framework of the buying cycle, deciding what to measure and how to measure comes down to putting ticks in the right boxes. Who selects those boxes and who needs to tick them brings us to the subject of *alignment.*

Why alignment matters

The term might sound like pretentious jargon, but alignment is, in fact, very important when it comes to measurement. It is particularly important when creating conversion ratings for your leads.

Alignment ensures that key players responsible for fulfilment are involved in the process of measurement – through deciding the parameters for your lead-quality indicators and the CR. This is significant because what and how you measure can't be decided in isolation.

For example, who defines an acceptable period for leads to remain in a particular phase? Who understands the cross-functional implications of what the lead requires and when it's required? And who understands how the buying decision will be made and who influences it?

- Input from *Sales* is obviously important, through defining the criteria that they think indicate a high-quality lead. Apart from Sales, here are some examples of the type of inputs you may well need from other departments when measuring lead quality and the all-important CR.
- *Finance*: Are the margins acceptable across all your product and service lines? What is the cost for stockholding to enable fulfilment? How does this affect profitability? Can we agree on payment terms? How can we best manage cash flows? How creditworthy is the lead?
- *Production*: How do roll-out milestones affect our capacity and scheduling? What is the maximum lead time we can work to? Can our suppliers keep up?
- *Technical and service*: Can we deploy enough of the right resources, at the right time? Can the customer?

Refer back to the list you drew up at the end of Chapter 8 about who is responsible for what in terms of delivering on the Big Five (response, service, time, quality and price). Now is the time to revisit and update it.

All of these inputs will have an impact on how you determine conversion ratings for your leads.

Results through alignment

All the departments listed above derive a common benefit from measurement: it forecasts demand and helps you decide how to respond efficiently.

At the same time, it reinforces commitment to 'marketing united' in a customer-centric drive to increase sales and margins, revenue and profits.

It also provides the CEO with an accurate insight into how well the entire company understands the overall market, how effectively it serves the factors that motivate buying, and where it must improve.

To improve marketing performance, you need to *respond* to the insights gained from measurement.

Improvement through measurement

Now you have to act upon your findings. Knowing what's wrong isn't worth much if you don't fix it!

Let's say that measurement shows that your channels are reaching the right audiences. You're creating awareness among the people who influence and make buying decisions. However, they aren't responding positively. They're not moving through the cycle. They're not *motivated* to buy. And the reason for this is that they don't value what you're offering. It's a case of right people, wrong message.

The solution? Change the content so that it speaks to what they *do* value. And make sure it's relevant to their position in the cycle.

You also need to consider whether the message directed at your prospect is too long and too complex – or perhaps too simplistic. Does it lack credibility? Or could it be that you are expecting too much from your CTAs?

The bottom line is if you don't measure, you don't know what's working and what's not working. And if you don't know, you can't begin to improve.

So the bottom line is exactly what we're looking at next.

WHY *LE ROI* IS KING:
MEASURING RETURN ON MARKETING SPEND

Measurement is not about proving ROI – it's about improving ROI. Once you can demonstrate direct links between marketing and the results it delivers – profitable sales – measuring the return on marketing costs gets easier.

MEASUREMENT IS NOT
ABOUT PROVING ROI –
IT'S ABOUT IMPROVING ROI

It is easy to measure costs. Whether it's producing and placing a print advert or staging a live event, the costs appear on the invoices from your suppliers; you merely have to add them up.

It's far harder to forge a direct link between those costs and the results they bring. It may be easy to allocate costs to vague notions such as brand awareness, thought leadership and customer engagement, but that's not good enough. This would be the sort of smoke-and-mirrors approach to ROI that undermines respect for marketing. It also makes it a lot harder to get the budget you need to increase revenue and profits.

Incredibly, 'revenue-driven marketing' and 'profit-driven marketing' are relatively new phrases in the world of B2B. The trademarked term 'revenue marketing', coined by The Pedowitz Group in 2010, describes today's B2B marketer as having 'some type of accountability for revenue'. Hm, just some type?

Only recently, in May 2014, Google started a high-profile commentary on the 'new' world of 'profit-driven marketing' on its 'Think with Google' platform.

Can it be that marketers are only now realising that they're in the business of generating sales and protecting margins? Perhaps one reason for this is that many marketers see the task of creating profitable sales as being somehow beneath them. Maybe they don't want to get their hands dirty in what they regard as the grubby business of selling and dealing with customers! It is hardly surprising, then, that marketers often seem to have a lousy reputation.

But let's get back to the positive point about measuring bangs for bucks. We already looked at how to create direct links between your content, the channels that deliver it, and revenue and profits. The key is how to integrate the ability to measure from the outset.

Every part of your marketing needs a built-in system of measurement that links it to profitable sales. Once you've put such a system in place, you can start allocating costs to results. You can then establish where the bucks are spent most profitably.

Setting targets and measuring progress towards them

If you accept that attracting and retaining profitable customers is marketing's purpose, then you need to set some related targets:

- *Numbers*: revenue and profit figures for specific products and services within specific market sectors
- *Time frames*: when the targets need to be reached
- *Budget*: how much you can spend to hit the targets
- *Authority*: removing any barriers to achieving your targets.

Authority is critically important. So some things may have to change: there may need to be a serious overhaul of how the business delivers on the Big Five buying motivators. In fact, you'll need to measure with muscle.

MEASURING WITH MUSCLE

Business men go down with their businesses because they like the old way so well they cannot bring themselves to change. One sees them all about — men who do not know that yesterday is past, and who woke up this morning with last year's ideas. – Henry Ford

What happens if the results from measuring your marketing performance demonstrate shortcomings within products, services and processes? Who is responsible for change? How will shortcomings be addressed, and then remeasured to assess the impact of improvements?

This might be CEO territory. Instigating and monitoring the necessary changes and presenting performance measurements can be a tricky task. And those with operational responsibilities may skate over findings:

- 'Quality control letting us down? No way!'
- 'They accuse us of uncompetitive lead times?! They think it's easy making this stuff?!'
- 'Changes to the website? Whatever for? Nobody visits!'
- 'Our prices aren't even in the ballpark — customers always say that!'

Some things may need to change

Top-level support to act upon your measurements is clearly essential. Securing that support becomes a lot easier if you can demonstrate a few of the benefits derived from measurement:

- improved understanding of customers' current and future needs — and how to meet them
- higher returns on correctly focused marketing spend
- anticipating future demand and scheduling responses
- forecasting revenue and profitability
- sidelining the competition.

And the biggest benefit:

- the ability to increase sales and reinforce margins by motivating your markets to buy — from you.

MEASURING WITH PURPOSE

> *If they can get you asking the wrong questions, they don't have to*
> *worry about answers.*
> — Thomas Pynchon, *Gravity's Rainbow*, 1973

This statement by Thomas Pynchon really sums up the measurement dilemma for today's B2B marketer. The rise of digital has, paradoxically, both compounded and eased this dilemma.

It has eased it by giving us access to a treasure trove of data that can be accessed in real time to give immediate insights into buying behaviour. But it's compounded the dilemma, because there's so much data that can be measured that it is hard to avoid analysis paralysis. Defining which data should be interpreted and what technique should be used to carry out the analysis is a job in its own right.

In addition, digital measurement has spawned two more buzz-phrases for marketing's jargon glossary: 'metrics' and 'analytics'. Surely, these must be good because now it sounds as if we're measuring scientifically?! In fact, it sounds as if we can automate the measurement process and provide accurate insights into marketing's performance. So we focus on what's easy to measure digitally and automatically.

We can track and record the digital activities of prospects. We measure web traffic by page views, and time-on-site. We can monitor conversations on social media and online user groups. We can capture who is downloading content from our websites, emails and newsletters. We can initiate and encourage dialogue with our digital CTAs. But page views and downloads, social sentiment and landing-page performance doesn't give you much insight unless you tie these data to a sales outcome.

Make sure it matters

The very danger of falling into the digital metrics trap is what Pynchon's quirky quote highlights. Unless you measure marketing performance against the benchmarks of sales and margins, you are not only measuring for the sake of measuring, you are measuring the wrong things. And then it really doesn't matter what the answers are!

To avoid this trap, we looked at ways of avoiding the myopia that often accompanies big data and offered guidance on determining which tactics deliver the best ROI (see Chapter 10: Digital, digital, digital). You might want to reread some of the tips in the context of conversion ratings and offline measurement.

We're almost done with measurement, but before we wrap up this chapter, we need to consider the significance of measuring market share.

MEASURING MARKET SHARE

Understanding market share will help you in one critical respect: it tells you how big the pie is. That's relevant because you can't bite fifty million bucks out of a forty-million-buck pie.

A note of caution regarding the use of market share as a performance benchmark: share can rise and fall, but these ups and downs don't necessarily have a negative effect on the key benchmarks of revenue and profits. That's because not all customers are profitable customers. In fact, you may well want to lose some: the bad payers, the ones who refuse to learn how to use your products and are constantly calling for support, and the ones who make demands on response, service, time, quality and price that nobody, anywhere, could ever meet – 'We need a cheap skateboard to take us to Mars next month.' In fact, you may want to offer these customers to your competitors as the proverbial Trojan Horse.

As for your profitable customers, you want as many of these as you can handle. You want a big share of them. This comes down to listing the criteria that define such customers.

All in all, quite reassuringly, if you look after sales and margins, market share tends to look after itself. In our final chapter, on results-based planning, we will now look at how you plan for more sales and stronger margins.

DIRECTIONS TO RESULTS

There are already several examples in this chapter of what to measure and how to measure it. We've covered how to measure the performance of your content, the channels that deliver it and the quality of your leads. So we won't repeat them here. But here are some more things you can do to achieve measurement success.

Directions to results for Chapter 11 will show you:
- *how to build measurements into all your marketing activities and link them to achievements*
- *how to formulate CTAs that actually create action.*

Follow these steps to get into the fast lane:
- Choose one item of your existing content (a brochure, product sheet or perhaps a case study). Does it have a clear CTA that is likely to create action? If not, why not? Now ask if the CTA can be linked to your chosen piece of content. And if not, why not?
- A CTA that merely says 'Please call us for more information' is pretty useless. 'Please call Jack to discuss how we can advance your success in managing xyz' is much better, because Jack will know where the call came from – and there's more motivation to call him. The CTA had an *identifier* and a *motivator*. This is what all your CTAs should contain. Now repeat this process for the rest of your content.
- Choose an activity – an advert, a press release or a live event. Before even thinking about what type of advert, press release or event, decide how you'll measure and record the results it's intended to produce.

- Build this approach into all your activities and you'll be measuring from the very start. You'll be creating direct links between activities and achievement. Most importantly, measurement will have set you on the path to improvement.
- Refer back to the list you drew up at the end of Chapter 8 to detail who is responsible for what in terms of the Big Five. Update this list, and remember to continue doing so.
- Also refer back to and update the reality check you did on customer expectations vs. customer experiences at the end of Chapter 8.

12

Results-based planning: building a fast track to profitable sales

HOW TO DEFINE THE STRATEGY AND
TACTICS THAT GENERATE RESULTS

Coming up in this chapter:
- You already have a plan
    - Putting your plan into action
    - The SMART way to target results
    - Making it happen: working with calendars, schedules and deadlines
    - Beware of being busy, busy, busy

YOU ALREADY HAVE A PLAN

Now for the shortest chapter of them all. It's not short because planning isn't important (in fact, it is critical if you want to get results). It is short because all the way through this book you've been planning to increase your sales, protect your margins and build your market share.

You now know how to:
- identify who influences and makes buying decisions
- reach them with relevant content
- prove that you create the value they need
- build their sales-creating trust in your brand
- motivate them to buy from you
- measure your sales-generating performance.

All of this means you already have a plan.

Now you simply need to put this plan into action. How you do that depends on the precise results you want to achieve.

Putting your plan into action

The first thing to remember when deciding how to implement your plan is to start with results. *What* you want to achieve always comes first. *How* to achieve it always comes second.

WHAT YOU WANT TO ACHIEVE ALWAYS COMES FIRST. *HOW* TO ACHIEVE IT COMES SECOND

Here are the three fantastic advantages of results-based planning:
1. It simplifies the process of deciding which actions you need to take to get your result.

2. It keeps everything very practical, particularly in terms of defining the resources you can draw upon (such as money, time and skills).

3. It lays the foundations for increasing your performance in ways that delight every CEO: by being more effective and more efficient. The process boils down to doing the right things in the right way. And: you now know what the right things are.

The SMART way to target results

'SMART' might be a bit of a tired old jargony acronym, but it's still a simple way to guide your thinking about what you want to achieve. You can define the results you're looking for in terms of these five SMART benchmarks:

- Specific
- Measurable
- Agreed
- Realistic
- Timelined.

When we looked at how to get results from PR in Chapter 9, we covered the importance of being really specific about the result you want to achieve. The result might be to increase sales of one product or service within a particular market sector. This needs to be measurable against the type of yardsticks that really matter: by what percentage must these sales increase and at what margin? This ticks off the first two benchmarks on your SMART list: *specific* and *measurable*.

You now want your actions to be supported by your colleagues. In terms of what you're planning, have they all *agreed* to deliver the sort of customer experience that will empower you to achieve the result? Can production meet demand? Can after-sales and support? Will the right stock be available? What will the lead times be? Is finance happy with the cash-flow implications and the pricing? All of this comes back to ensuring that marketing's purpose – to attract and retain profitable customers – is being served right across your business. As we saw in

Chapter 8 (Marketing united), everyone who affects the customer experience needs to be contributing to that purpose.

Now you need to check what resources you will need to implement your actions. You have to be *realistic* in terms of the skills you need to apply and all the costs involved in achieving your result.

Last on your SMART list is the *timeline*: when are the results going to come rolling in? It helps to be realistic about that too!

Making it happen: working with calendars, schedules and deadlines

Now that you've got a SMART definition of *what* result you want, you can begin thinking about *how* to achieve it. This is a pretty simple process: you identify the tasks to be performed, determine who is responsible for them, and by when they need to be completed. All this info can go into an activity schedule.

It also helps to set up a calendar with some fixed dates (deadlines for editorial features or adverts in relevant media, or for live events that are likely to attract influencers you want to reach). This means you do need to gather these kinds of calendar-based details from your chosen channels. You certainly don't want to work in the dark here.

Beware of being busy, busy, busy

Do not confuse activity with achievement! We've said this before, but it's worth remembering, and here's why: a lot of what's said about marketing (and there's a lot of it!) has zero direct connection with creating profitable sales.

DO NOT CONFUSE
ACTIVITY WITH ACHIEVEMENT!

Be aware of placing too much emphasis on tools and techniques – the newer the better. All the time we seem to hear about the 'next big breakthrough' in marketing methods that promises us a silver bullet that is more efficient than the one we read about last week. There's major emphasis on *how* we can do things.

The problem with this is that it makes activity appear more important than achievement; it's easy to lose sight of *what* things we should be doing.

The tools and techniques at your disposal might all be fabulously efficient, but that doesn't mean they're automatically effective. None of them will get results unless they get the right content to the right people at the right time.

TOOLS AND TECHNIQUES ARE ONLY EFFECTIVE IF THEY GET THE RIGHT CONTENT TO THE RIGHT PEOPLE AT THE RIGHT TIME

The focus on being efficient rather than effective is nothing new. There truly is no magic wand in the marketing toolbox. And there never has been. In his 1973 book, *Management: Tasks, Responsibilities, Practices*, Peter Drucker highlighted the dangers of an over-reliance on techniques and tools:

> *the emphasis is on techniques rather than on principles, on mechanics rather than on decisions, on tools rather than on results, and, above all, on efficiency of the part rather than on performance of the whole.*

In the context of results-based planning, the astonishing clarity and common-sense thinking of Peter Drucker says it all:
- define what results you want
- decide how to apply B2B's governing rules to achieve them
- measure your result-generating performance in order to improve it.

This wise advice will allow your how-to marketing plan pretty much to develop itself.

There's something else that Peter Drucker's 1973 comment tells us: the very essence of marketing is still the same today as it was over forty years ago. And that's why our closing thoughts (The Long Hello) look back on B2B's governing rules and their application in pursuit of marketing's purpose.

DIRECTIONS TO RESULTS

In terms of planning, the word 'strategy' is often used as an excuse to keep on doing the wrong things in a new way. What it should mean to you is how to make and implement plans that achieve a defined result: profitable sales. And planning for that is as easy as it gets.

Directions to results for Chapter 12 will show you how to:
- *implement a results-based plan*
- *develop a strategy (don't give up on having a strategy just yet!)*
- *plan on sidelining the competition.*

Follow these steps to get into the fast lane:
- Use some SMART thinking to choose a precise result you want to achieve. This means keeping it specific, measurable, agreed, realistic and timelined.
- Define what needs to be done to get your result. To keep you on track, link these activities to calendars, schedules and deadlines.
- Now think about how the competition will respond. This is a seriously important part of your planning. What is it about the result you're aiming for that they would battle to match? If you're getting results, they'll try to compete! You also need to work out how you will counter their likely response and stay one step ahead.
- Then repeat the process for the next result, and the next one, and the next one …

The Long Hello:
building market relationships
that create profitable sales

THE SALES FUNCTION MATTERS,
BUT MARKETING MATTERS MORE

Coming up in this chapter:
- What is the Long Hello?
  - Wrapping it all up: turning activity into achievement
  - How to build sales-creating trust: two steps to success
- Differentiate or die
  - Why it's critical to be seen to be different
  - The commodity trap – and how to avoid it
  - Reveal the 'evidence of difference'
- The threat of the net
  - Death of a (traditional) salesman
  - A requiem to one-to-one selling: the road warrior rides into the sunset
  - Be seen in all the right places
- People come and go, relationships end … but the Long Hello endures

WHAT IS THE LONG HELLO?

Wrapping it all up: turning activity into achievement

The Long Hello focuses all marketing activity on a single point of achievement: creating profitable sales.

It is the continuing dialogue that motivates customers to buy from you – and to keep on buying from you. In essence, this entire book deals with managing *your* Long Hello. It's about convincing everyone who influences buying decisions that they can *trust* the decisions they are taking.

Because in a B2B enterprise, nothing – absolutely nothing – matters more than building that sales-creating trust.

IN B2B NOTHING MATTERS MORE THAN BUILDING SALES-CREATING TRUST

How to build sales-creating trust: two steps to success

As we saw way back in Chapter 1 (The big, big market), the buying decisions that create your sales – what to buy, who to buy from and at what price – are typically influenced by many different people. A classic list of influencers might include industry analysts, specialist consultancies, media commentators, distributors, value-added resellers (VARs) and, of course, end-users.

Within the end-user group, the list becomes even longer and may cover finance, strategy, business analysis, IT, production, marketing, sales, HR, project management, R&D and customer support.

There are two steps to successfully creating this much-needed sales-creating trust: identify all the influencers, and then win their trust in order to create sales.

Step 1: Identify all the influencers

For major purchases – the ones that create major sales – people from different functions may come together as a formal decision-making unit. And they might be joined by external advisors for their specific expertise.

Whoever they are and whatever their job, when considering buying decisions, all influencers are motivated by the same two objectives:

- They each need to trust that their individual responsibilities will be fulfilled.
- They each need to trust that their professional success and the success of their organisation will be reinforced.

Before even thinking about issues such as buying motivators, marcoms messages, mapping content within the B2B buying cycle, communication channels, or measuring returns on marketing spend, you have to know exactly which influencers to reach, either directly or as a group with common interests.

If you skip this first step – or wing it using entrenched assumptions – there's simply no point in taking the second step: providing influencers with information that will win their trust.

Step 2: Win that sales-creating trust

Across the different influencers, how much do they each trust you to tick the boxes that matter most to them? And what's the basis for their trust?

To answer these questions, you will need to do a fast recap on how to link specific benefits to specific influencers.

So, let's say *reliability* is one of the benefits your products deliver. Perhaps this means low maintenance costs or increased productivity through reduced downtime. Maybe this particular characteristic of your products improves day-to-day operational efficiencies or strengthens the integrity of processes.

Reliability might produce all these different benefits, and more. This is great. But *who* benefits and *how* do they benefit? How does reliability help a distributor or a VAR? Why would it motivate a consultant's recommendation, or persuade an industry analyst or media commentator to express a positive opinion? From your end-users' perspective, which requirements are fulfilled by reliability?

In different ways, reliability might be a major plus for them all. If so, the combined weight of their positive perceptions needs to support a *unanimous* buying decision. In order to harness this united support, it is essential to ensure all influencers are exposed to relevant, credible information that specifically addresses their most pressing concerns.

That information – your content – must *prove* that each influencer's expectations will be matched by experiences. Your content has to prove that what is proposed will translate into what is provided.

YOUR CONTENT MUST PROVE THAT EACH INFLUENCER'S EXPECTATIONS WILL BE MATCHED BY EXPERIENCES

Content must be evidence – not flashy propaganda in which 'the large print giveth and the small print taketh away', as Tom Waits sang in the song 'Step right up'.

In Chapter 5 (Content is king!), we looked at how to create a content map based on each phase of the buying cycle. And in Chapter 7 (Extra special delivery), we looked at the typical questions buyers need to have answered in each phase – and how to deliver these answers to the right people.

You already know how to create relevant, credible content that reaches the right people at the right time. You know how to create positive perceptions right across the market. Here's why this is absolutely essential: if you operate in an environment where positive perceptions exist among all influencers, you logically have a much higher chance of creating profitable sales – everyone who matters agrees that the right buying decision is being made.

But that's not all. Such an environment also accelerates sales cycles. That's because decisions are quickly informed by trusted knowledge. This short-circuits the repetitive, time-consuming rigmarole of establishing new relationships with (previously unknown) influencers and responding to requests for the different sorts of information they need

– because your influencers already have the up-to-date information required to make their decisions.

While it might be unrealistic to expect that all influencers will be positive all the time, the underlying goal is to ensure that influential supporters outnumber – and outgun – any detractors.

This requires formal mechanisms to keep tabs on influencers and how they and their buying-decision criteria may change. This is because the buying environment does change. Influencers move on or up, and market forces alter in response to economic pressures, or as a result of technology advances or the way they are applied.

You also know how to keep records – and keep them current – using the *personas* we dealt with in Chapter 7 (Extra special delivery).

If you take these two straightforward steps, you will be reaching the right people with the right messages. You will be building sales-creating trust by saying the Long Hello.

The result of all this? Your activity will turn into achievement. Profitable sales will be created by the very people who influence and make the decisions about what to buy, who to buy from and at what price.

DIFFERENTIATE OR DIE

Why it's critical to be seen to be different

'Differentiate or die' – American marketing consultant Jack Trout wasn't being glib when he made this emphatic statement. It highlights the blunt fact that if customers can't tell the difference between you and the competition, then rock-bottom prices are your only hope for survival.

Every B2B company would like to charge higher prices and earn higher margins. But if your products and services appear to be no different from the competition, customers naturally battle to decide who to buy from. This means that they'll base their decision on price – and they'll be buying the cheapest.

If you compare companies competing for sales in the same B2B markets, they often look pretty much like clones of each other. If you look like a clone, you will have to overcome a high barrier to protecting margins, retaining customers and attracting new business.

Things get even worse when competing companies all speak the same jargon. They don't merely look alike, they even sound alike. The corporate ICT market is a prime example. Tech companies typically provide 'innovative, world-class solutions that combine best-of-breed products with best practices to deliver bespoke synergies through holistic partnerships that mitigate risk and add comprehensive value in converged value-chains. It's a world in which core competencies are harnessed to address key imperatives for all stakeholders. Where thought leadership is leveraged to deploy next-generation solutions via agile, cutting-edge methodologies that yield competitive advantage. And continuous improvement is achieved end-to-end with seamlessly integrated turnkey projects that are dynamic, flexible, adaptable, scalable, modular and future-proof.'

See what I mean? An entire sector has been infected by meaningless buzz-phrases. Their marketing sounds as if they've all sat down with a copy of the buzz-phrase generator I mentioned in Chapter 2 and used it to build their content: 'Right, pick three numbers! Oooh, that sounds good. And that one really does make us seem important. The punters will fall for this! What do *they* know?!' By describing themselves with this sort of identical-sounding gobbledegook, companies create a rod for their own backs: they allow price to become their only visible differentiator. When that happens, there is one rule only: price must be low.

The commodity trap – and how to avoid it

Aside from simply refusing to portray your company as a clone, the task of differentiating yourself from competitors includes a more challenging problem: commoditisation.

In globalised markets, where customers can source products from Bulgaria to Brazil, there is a growing similarity between the features and specifications of even the most sophisticated products and services.

Increasingly, they're seen by customers as being no more distinct than basic goods such as plastic bags or paper plates. When products and services are perceived as essentially the same – as commodities – customers will always look for the lowest price.

For undifferentiated suppliers, this means suffering the inevitable damage of being forced to sell on price: deals either get done at painfully low margins or get lost to cheaper competitors. Contracts worth millions can and actually *do* get lost over relatively tiny amounts.

If you focus on promoting features and specifications only, you run the risk of falling into a *commodity trap* that puts constant pressure on your pricing. In essence, this commodity trap is created when companies promote what they do instead of what they *do for customers*; in other words, when they're product-centric instead of customer-centric.

To avoid the commodity trap, it is essential to convince customers *how* you are different from the competition, and *why* those differences make it worth paying a higher price.

Reveal the 'evidence of difference'

So the big question is: How should a B2B company differentiate itself? Despite appearances to the contrary, all companies are different. Just like people, no two companies are exactly the same. They differ in how they provide their markets with relevant and credible answers to the big, basic questions listed in Chapter 2: Who are you? What do you do? And why do you matter – to me, the customer?

It is critical that you answer these questions in a customer-centric manner, because your answers reveal the 'evidence of difference'. And that evidence is important. Does the customer care whether you've been in business for a hundred years? What's the relevance of your manufacturing facilities, processes or quality controls? Why does your skills base and sector experience matter? What is the significance of your stockholding? Where is the value in your after-sales support?

Identifying and promoting the evidence of difference lies at the very heart of creating profitable sales at premium prices.

Unless you can *prove* to customers how these differences will contribute *directly* to their success, customers don't give two hoots whether you were founded in the year dot, have ultra-modern factories, run kanban systems, are ISO-whatever certified, hire top talent, operate extensively in their sector, hold big inventories or provide nationwide 24/7 service. Unless they can clearly see how any of this creates value for them – how it contributes directly to their success – they *won't* pay a premium for your products and services.

When they know no better, customers simply go for the rock-bottom clone price. And who can blame them?

So you need to think really hard about how you differ from your competition and *why* that matters to your customers. You need to spell this out very clearly so that customers know exactly how you create more *value* than your competitors.

THE THREAT OF THE NET

Death of a (traditional) salesman

B2B revenues and profitability are no longer driven exclusively by traditional sales teams.

In today's digitally centred business environment, the influence of sales teams is being rapidly replaced by the influence of the internet. Here's a quick reminder as to why this is happening and the challenges it has created.

In every B2B company, the single most important task is to generate profitable sales. For decades, this crucial task was entrusted to professional sales teams – to the mighty key-account managers and to the road warriors doing the miles from customer to customer.

They were in control. They really were. That's because they controlled the flow of sales-motivating information to customers – features, specifications, product reports, industry insights and latest opinions, testimonials, cost-benefit analyses and pricing. For customers and prospects, sales teams were the primary information source that informed buying decisions.

Their role was to build the one-to-one relationships that influenced buying decisions. They guided customers all the way through the buying cycle from the point of initial interest to their signing on the dotted line.

This long-established role is rapidly becoming less and less significant. In Chapter 5 (Content is king!), we saw how customers' behaviour within the buying cycle has changed fundamentally.

THE BUYING CYCLE HASN'T CHANGED; THE WAY CUSTOMERS BEHAVE IN IT HAS

The cycle itself hasn't changed, but the way customers behave in it certainly has. All because the internet has matured into a trusted resource. Digitally savvy customers are confident in using it to form opinions of products, services and suppliers – online and on their own. They research products, services and vendors on the web. And more and more, their buying decisions are guided by online user forums and special-interest groups.

A requiem to one-to-one selling: the road warrior rides into the sunset

The internet has created business buyers that are self-sold because they are self-advised. Prospects and customers no longer need or want extensive inputs from salespeople. They don't want to be sold to. They expect to sell to themselves.

So their first direct contact with a sales team may simply be to confirm prices and lead times. They have already digitally decided what they want. And who they want it from.

Right or wrong, they trust the advice they give themselves, and there's little chance to change their minds. The result of this is that the traditional sales function has been shoved right to the end of the buying cycle.

That's where major problems can start. When self-informed customers get that far down the decision-making road – on their own – their opinions and intentions have become embedded. This can create formidable barriers to closing deals. The reason for this? Unless you used the right channels to reach the right people with the right information in the cycle's opening phases, customers can easily form unrealistic expectations of the Big Five (response, service, time, quality and price) that cannot be met. Now your sales team is plagued with difficulties, as altering a prospect's expectations this late in the buying cycle is almost impossible. Negotiations can quickly become bogged down in reappraisals and revisions. Momentum and time are lost as customers have to step back and reassess their expectations.

In their search for someone to fulfil their digitally derived expectations, they start talking to more and more suppliers. The uncertainty and confusion caused by all this rethinking means that pricing can easily become the dominant factor in a buying decision. This road usually leads to lost sales or lower margins.

Be seen in all the right places

The influence of the internet also creates barriers to profitable sales if you're *not* visible, relevant and credible in the digital arena right from the beginning of the cycle. You can't beat the competition when you're out of sight and therefore out of mind. Customers and prospects who don't find the information that advances their buying decisions will look to find it elsewhere. That's also where their money will go: elsewhere.

PEOPLE COME AND GO, RELATIONSHIPS END ...
BUT THE LONG HELLO ENDURES

When your Long Hello inspires universal trust in your products and services, you don't have to sell. Once the market has convinced itself, you don't have to persuade it to buy. All you have to do is make the buying process as easy as possible.

Of course, having earned that sales-creating trust, you have to continue to deserve it in order to retain it. That's why it's called the *Long Hello*.

And as we said in Chapter 6 (Brands and branding), you have to walk your talk and deliver on your promises.

It's not that the sales relationship doesn't matter: people still buy from people and customers still enjoy that personal relationship. But they aren't buying the people. They are buying what they represent. They are buying your Long Hello because of all the ways in which it contributes to their success.

People come and go. They move on from customers and they move on from your team. Relationships can come to an end for various reasons.

But the Long Hello remains.

It creates the expectations that motivate buying and it delivers the experiences that meet them.

Your sales, your margins and your market share are all created by your Long Hello. Make sure you are saying it. And make sure your markets trust it.